《研究生英语读写教程》教学执行计划

Teacher's Manual for English Reading and Writing for Postgraduates

主　编　林　易　任永山　陈　聪
副主编　曲婧华　李艳霞　张娅丽
王　臻　李丙午

上海交通大学出版社

内容提要

本书是《研究生英语读写教程》(以下简称教程)的配套教师用书,学生或其他英语爱好者也可将其作为教程自学的辅导用书。本书对应教程的9个单元,内容涉及计算机、无线通信、卫星导航、物联网、人工智能、比特币、大数据、量子计算和深度学习,从教学内容、教学方法、组织过程、重点难点等方面对单元课文的教授进行了总体设计和详细安排。

图书在版编目(CIP)数据

《研究生英语读写教程》教学执行计划/林易,任永山,陈聪主编. —上海:上海交通大学出版社,2020

ISBN 978-7-313-23428-5

Ⅰ.①研… Ⅱ.①林…②任…③陈… Ⅲ.①英语—阅读教学—研究生—教学参考资料②英语—写作—研究生—教学参考资料 Ⅳ.①H319.39

中国版本图书馆CIP数据核字(2020)第110141号

《研究生英语读写教程》教学执行计划

《YANJIUSHENG YINGYU DUXIE JIAOCHENG》JIAOXUE ZHIXING JIHUA

主 编:林 易 任永山 陈 聪

出版发行:上海交通大学出版社　　地 址:上海市番禺路951号

邮政编码:200030　　电 话:021-64071208

印 制:苏州市古得堡数码印刷有限公司　　经 销:全国新华书店

开 本:787mm×1092mm 1/16　　印 张:10.5

字 数:243千字

版 次:2020年8月第1版　　印 次:2020年8月第1次印刷

书 号:ISBN 978-7-313-23428-5

定 价:68.00元

前　言

为了帮助教师更好规范课堂教学内容、设计课堂教学活动并提高课堂教学效果，我们编写了本教学执行计划，供教授《研究生英语读写教程》的教师参考使用。

《研究生英语读写教程》内容选自原版英文书籍、报纸、杂志、电子文献资料等，涉及计算机、无线通信、卫星导航、物联网、人工智能、比特币、大数据、量子计算、深度学习等近几年最为热门的一些专业领域。选文题材新颖，语言规范，不仅关注读者对科技和专业知识的需求，还具备一定的思辨性和启发性。研究生通过学习该教程，可以为下一步的专业英语阅读、写作和交流打下坚实的基础。

本教学执行计划在编写过程中坚持以下基本教学理念和指导思想：

首先，强调语言根基夯实。词汇是构成语言最基本的单位，扩充词汇量是提高学生英语能力的前提。我们从音、形、义、用四个方面讲解课文的重点词汇和短语，词义的解释既有英文也有中文，选自课文的例句均标注其在文中出现的段落，便于教学中结合上下文让学生真正掌握这些词汇、短语的用法。难句解析包括英文释义、解析和翻译，通过这些训练，教师可以帮助学生更加透彻理解难句结构、扩大并熟练掌握词汇、梳理巩固已学语法知识。

其次，着眼科技素养提升。教程选材来自时下一些热门的科技领域，涉及不少专业表述、概念、技术和应用等，给缺乏专业背景的语言教师组织教学活动带来了一定难度。因此，我们在背景知识部分对这方面内容进行了汇总，有利于教师更好地指导学习者了解学科前沿动态，熟悉专业术语和相关概念，并提高对科技文献的阅读理解能力和思辨能力。

最后，突出应用技能培养。对于研究生来说，语言应用是语言学习最主要的目的，因此在设计教学活动时，要结合研究生善于独立思考和自主学习的特点，突出语言应用技能的培养。篇章分析和写作技巧两个部分，就是以知识输出为驱动，通过启发式、探究式、任务式、讨论式等多种形式的教学活动，强化口语输出和写作输出两个重要技能的培养。在组织篇章分析时，学生可以分组讨论，绘制思维导图并进行口头陈述；而写作技巧部分旨在结合课文，通过实例学习学术英语写作的基本特点和技巧，再配套实践练习加以巩固。

由于水平有限，错漏之处在所难免，恳请广大读者提出宝贵意见。

编者

Contents

Unit One
Computer Technology

Section A Vanishing Point: The Rise of the Invisible Computer

文章主旨

Since 1965, Moore's law has had a great influence on the entire computing industry. But now Moore's law is near its end with the rapid development of modern science. However, the end of Moore's law does not mean that the computer revolution will stall since many new technologies can be adopted to make computers faster. Moore's law may soon be over, but the computing revolution is not.

教学目标

- To learn the future development of computer and its related technologies.
- To master the technical words and expressions related to computing science.
- To be able to use the knowledge learned to discuss issues about computing science.

学习时间

4 hours (2 hours for the text; 2 hours for discussion)

A. 课堂讲授模块

预习要求

- To learn and recite the new words.
- To grasp the main idea of the text after reading.
- To search for materials related to computing science.

学习时间

2 hours

教学方法

heuristic teaching; project-based teaching; task-driven teaching; group discussion; self-study and peer learning

组织形式

- Let the students work in groups to discuss the structure and main idea of the text based on fast reading, and to draw a simple mind-map as well.
- Summarize key technical terms, words and phrases, and sentence patterns in the article involving Moore's law, Dennard scaling, 3D chips, quantum computing, cloud computing, IoT, etc.
- Let students discuss in groups the gains based on their fields of research, and a presentation is expected.
- Analyze the complex sentences and technical issues. Spare some time to respond to any questions from students.

背景知识

1. Moore's law

Moore's law (摩尔定律) refers to the observation that the number of transistors in a dense integrated circuit doubles about every two years. The observation is named after Gordon Moore, the co-founder of Fairchild Semiconductor and Intel, whose 1965 paper described a doubling every year in the number of components per integrated circuit, and projected this rate of growth would continue for at least another decade. In 1975, looking forward to the next decade, he revised the forecast to doubling every two years.

2. Moore's second law

Moore's second law (摩尔第二定律), named for Gordon Moore, says that the cost of a semiconductor chip fabrication plant doubles every four years. As of 2015, the price had already reached about 14 billion U.S. dollars.

Moore's second law can be seen as the economic flip side to Moore's (first) law—that the number of transistors in a dense integrated circuit doubles every two years. The latter is a direct consequence of the ongoing growth of the capital-intensive semiconductor industry—innovative and popular products mean more profits, meaning more capital available to invest in ever higher levels of large-scale integration, which in turn leads to creation of even more innovative products.

The semiconductor industry has always been extremely capital-intensive, with ever-dropping manufacturing unit costs. Thus, the ultimate limits to growth of the industry will constrain the maximum amount of capital that can be invested in new products; at some point, Moore's second law will collide with Moore's Law.

It has been suggested that fabrication plant costs have not increased as quickly as predicted by Moore's second law—indeed plateauing in the late 1990s—and also that the fabrication plant cost per transistor (which has shown a pronounced downward trend) may be more relevant as a constraint on Moore's Law.

3. Dennard scaling

Dennard scaling (登纳德缩放比例定律), also known as MOSFET scaling, is a scaling law based on a 1974 paper co-authored by Robert H. Dennard, after whom it is named. Originally formulated for MOSFETs, it states, roughly, that as transistors get smaller their power density stays constant, so that the power use stays in proportion with area: both voltage and current scale (downward) with length.

Dennard scaling relates to Moore's law (which postulates a reduction in the size of transistors leading to more and more transistors per chip at the cost-effective optimum) and claims that the performance per watt of computing is growing exponentially at roughly the same rate. This is closely related to Koomey's law, which says that performance per watt in computing has been doubling every 1.57 years (somewhat faster than the doubling period of Moore's law, which is about 2 years).

4. Intel

Intel (英特尔) is an American multinational corporation and technology company headquartered in Santa Clara, California (colloquially referred to as "Silicon Valley") that was founded by Gordon Moore (of Moore's law fame) and Robert Noyce. It is the world's largest and highest valued semiconductor chip maker based on revenue, and is the inventor of the x86 series of microprocessors: the processors found in most personal computers (PCs). Intel supplies processors for computer system manufacturers such as Apple, Lenovo, HP, and Dell. Intel also manufactures motherboard chipsets, network interface controllers and integrated circuits, flash memory, graphics chips, embedded processors and other devices related to communications and computing.

5. Taiwan Semiconductor Manufacturing Company

Taiwan Semiconductor Manufacturing Company (TSMC) (台积电) pioneered the pure-play foundry business model when it was founded in 1987, and has been the world's largest dedicated semiconductor foundry ever since. The company supports a thriving ecosystem of global customers and partners with the industry's leading process technology and portfolio of design enablement solutions to unleash innovation for the global semiconductor industry.

TSMC serves its customers with global capacity of about 13 million 12-inch equivalent wafers per year in 2020, and provides the broadest range of technologies from 2 micron all the way to foundry's most advanced processes, which is 7-nanometer today. TSMC is the first foundry to provide 7-nanometer production capabilities and the first to commercialize Extreme Ultraviolet （EUV） lithography technology in delivering customer products to market in high volume. TSMC is headquartered in Hsinchu, Taiwan of China.

重点词汇

1. **obscure** /əbˈskjʊə(r)/ *adj*. 1)If something or someone is obscure, they are unknown, or are known by only a few people. 鲜为人知的；2)Something that is obscure is difficult to understand or deal with, usually because it involves so many parts or details. 复杂难懂的，难处理的
   - ➢ In 1971, Intel, then an ***obscure*** firm in what would only later come to be known as Silicon Valley, released a chip called the 4004. (Para. 1)
   - ➢ The origin of the custom is ***obscure***.
   - ➢ The contracts are written in ***obscure*** language.
2. **feature** /ˈfiːtʃə(r)/ *n*. A feature of something is an interesting or important part or characteristic of it. 特点；*v*. When something such as a film or exhibition features a particular person or thing, they are an important part of it. (电影等)由……主演，(展览会等)以……为重点
   - ➢ Shrinking a chip's components gets harder each time you do it, and with modern transistors having ***features*** measured in mere dozens of atoms, engineers are simply running out of room. (Para. 5)
   - ➢ Modern chips are starting to ***feature*** specialized circuits designed to speed up common tasks ... (Para. 12)
   - ➢ Patriotic songs have long been a ***feature*** of Kuwaiti life.
   - ➢ The hour-long program will be updated each week and ***feature*** highlights from recent games.
3. **erode** /ɪˈrəʊd/ *v*. 1)If rock or soil erodes or is eroded by the weather, sea, or wind, it cracks and breaks so that it is gradually destroyed. 侵蚀；2)If someone's authority, right, or confidence erodes or is eroded, it is gradually destroyed or removed. 削弱［正式］；3) If the value of something erodes or is eroded by something such as inflation or age, its value decreases. 降低
   - ➢ At the same time, the rising cost of the ultra-sophisticated equipment needed to make the chips is ***eroding*** the financial gains. (Para. 7)
   - ➢ The storm washed away buildings and roads and ***eroded*** beaches.
   - ➢ His critics say his fumbling on the issue of reform has ***eroded*** his authority.
   - ➢ Competition in the financial marketplace has ***eroded*** profits.
4. **consensus** /kənˈsensəs/ *n*. A consensus is general agreement among a group of people. 共识
   - ➢ The result is a ***consensus*** among Silicon Valley's experts that Moore's law is near

its end. (Para. 8)

➢ The ***consensus*** among the world's scientists is that the world is likely to warm up over the next few decades.

5. **stall** /stɔːl/ *v*. If a process stalls, or if someone or something stalls it, the process stops but may continue at a later time. 使暂停;暂停

➢ The end of Moore's law does not mean that the computer revolution will ***stall***. (Para. 9)

➢ Social Democratic Party has vowed to try to ***stall*** the bill until the current session ends.

6. **incentive** /ɪnˈsentɪv/ *n*. If something is an incentive to do something, it encourages you to do it. 激励,动机,鼓励

➢ The fact that their customers would be buying faster machines every few years weakened the ***incentive*** even further. (Para. 11)

➢ The state provides financial ***incentives*** for film production.

7. **boost** /buːst/ *v*. If one thing boosts another, it causes it to increase, improve, or be more successful. 促进;*n*. an increase or improvement 促进,增强

➢ Specialized circuitry will provide a significant ***boost***. (Para. 12)

➢ Lower interest rates can ***boost*** the economy by reducing borrowing costs for consumers and businesses.

➢ The brake system utilizes hydraulic pressure for power ***boost***.

8. **reckon** /ˈrekən/ *v*. If you reckon that something is true, you think that it is true. 想,认为

➢ IBM ***reckons*** that 3D chips could allow designers to shrink a supercomputer that currently fills a building to something the size of a shoebox. (Para. 14)

➢ Some studies ***reckon*** inequality is mildly bad for growth.

9. **exotic** /ɪgˈzɒtɪk/ *adj*. Something that is exotic is unusual and interesting, usually because it comes from or is related to a distant country. (常因来自遥远的他国而显得)奇异的

➢ There are more ***exotic*** ideas, too. (Para. 16)

➢ They spend a few weeks every year photographing ***exotic*** wildlife overseas.

10. **intractable** /ɪnˈtræktəbl/ *adj*. Intractable problems or situations are very difficult to deal with. 棘手的[正式]

➢ ... a problem that has thousands of uses in manufacturing and industry but that conventional machines find almost completely ***intractable***. (Para. 16)

➢ The economy still faces ***intractable*** problems.

11. **conceivable** /kənˈsiːvəbl/ *adj*. If something is conceivable, you can imagine it or believe it. 可想象的,可相信的

➢ Dubbed the Internet of Things (IoT), the idea is to embed computing into almost every ***conceivable*** object. (Para. 22)

➢ Without their support, the project would not have been ***conceivable***.

重点短语

1. **figure out**: If you figure out a solution to a problem or the reason for something, you succeed in solving it or understanding it. 想出,弄明白[非正式]

   ➢ Each year, firms such as Intel and the Taiwan Semiconductor Manufacturing Company spend billions of dollars ***figuring out*** how to keep shrinking the components that go into computer chips. (Para. 4)

   ➢ Some study is needed to ***figure out*** the best approach.

   ➢ They're trying to ***figure out*** the politics of this whole situation.

2. **shell out**: If you shell out for something, you spend a lot of money on it. 付(一大笔钱)[非正式]

   ➢ Chips with smaller components, in other words, are better chips, which is why the computing industry has been able to persuade consumers to ***shell out*** for the latest models every few years. (Para. 6)

   ➢ An insurance policy will save you from having to ***shell out*** for repairs.

   ➢ Last year voters ***shelled out*** $110 million in general-election funds.

3. **wind down**: If someone winds down a business or activity, they gradually reduce the amount of work that is done or the number of people that are involved, usually before closing or stopping it completely. 逐步减少(业务或活动等直至停止)

   ➢ As Moore's law ***winds down***, the famously short product cycles of the computing industry may start to lengthen, giving programmers more time to polish their work. (Para. 11)

   ➢ The solution is to ***wind down*** the leverage over time, not to increase it.

   ➢ The war is ***winding down*** and the inevitable end is coming.

4. **seal off**: to make tight; to secure against leakage 封闭

   ➢ For a quantum computer to work, its internals must be ***sealed off*** from the outside world. (Para. 17)

   ➢ The downtown area is ***sealed off*** by police barricades.

   ➢ Police ***sealed off*** the area and evacuated some people.

5. **on demand**: according to the requirements 根据需求

   ➢ In other words, computing will become a utility that is tapped ***on demand***, like electricity or water today. (Para. 19)

   ➢ It allows storage administrators to allocate storage ***on demand***.

   ➢ Research suggests that feeding ***on demand*** has psychological benefits.

难句解析

1. It was a marvel of its time, built from 2,300 tiny transistors, each around 10,000

nanometers (or billionths of a meter) across—about the size of a red blood cell. (Para. 1)

Paraphrase: The chip is composed of 2,300 tiny transistors, each of which is around 10,000 nanometers (or billionths of a meter) across—about the size of a red blood cell. Therefore, it was regarded as a miracle of its time.

解析：全句由一个主句 It was a marvel of its time，再加两个状语 built from 2,300 tiny transistors, each around 10,000 nanometers (or billionths of a meter) across 和一个同位语 about the size of a red blood cell 组成。其中，第一个状语由过去分词短语 built 构成，第二个状语由独立主格构成，详细补充说明这款芯片的具体特点，实质上是解释为什么它被誉为这个时代的奇迹。最后又使用同位语让读者更清晰地认识到每个晶体管到底小到何种程度。很多短语，如形容词短语、现在分词短语、过去分词短语、介词短语、副词短语等都可以用作状语，补充说明主语的特点、状态、动作等，如：

- ***Spaced 14 nanometers apart***, each is so tiny as to be literally invisible, for they are more than an order of magnitude smaller than the wavelengths of light that humans use to see. (Para. 2) 每个晶体管之间间隔 14 纳米，体积非常小，肉眼不可见，因为它们比人类能够看到的光的波长小一个数量级。
- Shrinking a chip's components gets harder each time you do it, and ***with modern transistors having features measured in mere dozens of atoms***, engineers are simply running out of room. (Para. 5) 每次缩小芯片元件都会变得愈加困难，并且因为现代晶体管只有几十个原子大小，工程师们完全没有改进的空间。
- ***Accurate in operation and high in speed***, computers have found wide use in every field.
- I stand here today, ***humbled by the task before us***, ***grateful for the trust you have bestowed***, ***mindful of the sacrifices borne by our ancestors***.
- ***At 2,473 meters***, it is the highest mountain pass in Europe.

翻译：这块芯片是这个时代的奇迹，由 2 300 个微小的晶体管构成，每个晶体管直径大约 10 000 纳米(或十亿分之一米)——大约相当于一个红细胞的大小。

2. Along the way, Moore's law has helped to build a world in which chips are built in to everything from kettles to cars (which can, increasingly, drive themselves), where millions of people relax in virtual worlds, financial markets are played by algorithms, and pundits worry that artificial intelligence will soon take all the jobs. (Para. 4)

Paraphrase: Along this direction, with the help of Moore's law, a world has been built. In this world, chips are inserted into everything from kettles to cars (increasing number of cars can realize self-driving). And in this world, millions of people relax themselves in virtual worlds, and algorithms take the charge of financial markets. Experts fear that artificial intelligence will soon take the place of people to do all the jobs.

解析：此句为并列复合句，主干部分为一个并列句 Moore's law has helped to build a world . . . and pundits worry that artificial intelligence will soon take all the jobs，并列句的前半部分插入了两个从句：一个是由 in which 引导的非限制性定语从句，解释说明这是一个什么样的世界；另一个是由 where 引导的状语从句，说明在这个世界中人们是如何生活的，金融市场是如何运作的。

翻译：沿着这条道路，摩尔定律已经帮助我们建立了一个世界。在这个世界中，从水壶到汽车(越来越多的汽车可以实现自动驾驶)，每一样物品都嵌入了芯片，数以百万计的人们在虚拟世界中放松身心，金融市场通过算法来运行。专家们担心人工智能将很快承担所有的工作。

3. But it is also a force that is nearly spent. (Para. 5)

Paraphrase：But Moore's law almost exerts its full potential. It may soon be over.

解析：此句难点主要在于短语 be spent 的理解，指的是 be exhausted。

翻译：但是这种力量也差不多耗尽了。

4. For the law to hold until 2050 means there will have to be 17 more, in which case those engineers would have to figure out how to build computers from components smaller than an atom of hydrogen, the smallest element there is. (Para. 5)

Paraphrase：Making Moore's law continue to work until 2050 means there will be 17 more cycles. In this case, those engineers would have to work out how to build computers from components smaller than an atom of hydrogen, which is the smallest element in the world.

解析：此句中有一个由 in which 引导的非限制性定语从句，非限制性定语从句中还有一个同位语，解释说明氢原子的特点。

翻译：为了使摩尔定律的效力一直持续到 2050 年，这意味着还要再增加 17 个周期。在这种情况下，工程师们必须想出办法，如何用比氢原子(世界上最小的元素)还小的部件来制造电脑。

5. Yet business will kill Moore's law before physics does, for the benefits of shrinking transistors are not what they used to be. (Para. 6)

Paraphrase：However, since shrinking transistors will not bring so many financial gains as it used to, Moore's law will be killed due to the decrease in financial benefits rather than the exhaustion of physical technology.

解析：此句主要理解 business will kill Moore's law before physics does 的含义。结合上下文，business 在这指的是商业利益层面，而 physics 指的是技术层面。

翻译：然而，商业将比物理学更早地扼杀摩尔定律，因为压缩晶体管体积带来的好处已今非昔比。

6. Moore's law was given teeth by a related phenomenon called "Dennard scaling" (named for Robert Dennard, an IBM engineer who first formalized the idea in 1974), which states that shrinking a chip's components makes that chip faster, less power-hungry and cheaper to produce. (Para. 6)

Paraphrase：Moore's law was helped by a related phenomenon called "Dennard scaling" (named for Robert Dennard, an IBM engineer who first put forward the idea in 1974). "Dennard scaling" states that compressing a chip's components makes that chip faster, less power consumptive and with lower production cost.

解析：本句有一个 which 引导的非限制性定语从句，解释什么是 Dennard scaling（登纳德缩放比例定律）。括号中有一个由 who 引导的定语从句修饰的同位语 an IBM engineer。本句的难点在于短语 be given teeth 的理解，可以翻译为"助力"。

翻译：被称为"登纳德缩放比例定律"的相关现象（以 1974 年首次正式提出该想法的 IBM 工程师 Robert Dennard 的名字命名）使摩尔定律如虎添翼。"登纳德缩放比例定律"指出缩小芯片组件会使芯片速度更快、耗电更少且生产成本更低。

7. One of the most powerful technological forces of the past 50 years, in other words, will soon have run its course. The assumption that computers will carry on getting better and cheaper at breakneck speed is baked into people's ideas about the future. (Para. 9)

Paraphrase：In other words, Moore's law, which is one of the most powerful technological forces in the past 50 years, will soon come to an end. People assume that in the future computers will get better and cheaper at high speed.

解析：本主的主要难点在于短语 run its course, be baked into people's ideas 的理解。run its course 可以理解为 come to an end, be baked into people's ideas 可以理解为 people hold the idea。

➢ Another small rate increase may come later in the year, but overall, the current round of tightening may soon have ***run its course***, many believe. 今年晚些时候可能会有另一次小幅度的利率上调。但是，许多人相信本轮的紧缩可能很快便会结束。

翻译：换句话说，过去 50 年最强大的技术力量之一将很快走到尽头。计算机将以极快的速度变得更好、更便宜的假设已经深入人们对未来的认知中。

8. There are some easy wins. (Para. 11)

Paraphrase：There are some easy methods to make computers faster and cheaper.

解析：本句主要难点在于对 easy wins 的理解。

➢ There are some tips in the book that can produce an ***easy win*** for the customer. 书中有一些秘诀，能够轻松为客户带来益处。

翻译：要想提高计算机的速度还有一些轻松的方法。

9. Self-driving cars, for instance, will increasingly make use of machine vision, in which computers learn to interpret images from the real world, classifying objects and extracting information, which is a computationally demanding task. (Para. 12)

Paraphrase：For example, self-driving cars will increasingly take the advantage of machine vision, in which computers learn to interpret images from the real world, classify objects and extract information. This task is computationally demanding.

解析：本句有两个非限制性定语从句。第一个 in which 指的是 in machine vision，第二个 which 指的是 to learn to interpret images from the real world，classifying objects and extracting information。注意句中两个现在分词短语的使用，现在分词短语经常用在主句后，表示伴随、并列的动作。举例如下：

➢ This paper gives an overview of GRASP，***describing its basic components and enhancements to the basic procedure***.

➢ This paper discusses the need and possible forms of human interfaces to Internet services，***challenging the common notion that Internet services are simply computer-computer systems***.

此外，现在分词短语在主句后，也常常表示结果。举例如下：

➢ As Moore's law winds down，the famously short product cycles of the computing industry may start to lengthen，***giving programmers more time to polish their work***.（Para.11）

➢ Modern chips already run hot，***requiring beefy heatsinks and fans to keep them cool***.（Para.15）

➢ Trillions of tiny chips will be scattered through every corner of the physical environment，***making a world more comprehensible and more monitored than ever before***.（Para.27）

翻译：例如，自动驾驶汽车将越来越多地利用机器视觉。其中，计算机学习如何解析来自现实世界的图像，把目标分类，并且提取信息，这种任务对计算要求相当高。

10. Their most famous application is cracking some cryptographic codes，but their most important use may be accurately simulating the quantum subtleties of chemistry，a problem that has thousands of uses in manufacturing and industry but that conventional machines find almost completely intractable.（Para.16）

Paraphrase：The most famous application of quantum computing is to break some cryptographic codes，but accurately simulating the quantum subtleties of chemistry may be their most important application，which can be widely used in manufacturing and industry. But it is impossible to use conventional machines to make the simulation.

解析：本句主要难点在于 problem 后面有一个定语从句 that has thousands of uses in manufacturing and industry，同时，后面还有一个同位语从句 but that conventional computers find almost completely intractable。

同位语从句和定语从句都放在被修饰词的后边，从形式上和作用上来看，它们都非常相似。实际上，二者区别很大。我们可以从如下几个方面进行区分：

1）从句与先行词的关系

从语义角度看，同位语从句与先行词之间存在的是同位或等同的关系，而定语从句与先行词之间存在的是所属关系，表示"……的"，起修饰限定作用。

➢ The news *that* she had passed the exam made her parents very happy.（同位语从

句,that 之后是 news 的具体内容)

- The news ***that*** he told us interested all of us.(定语从句,that 之后是对 news 的解释)

2) 引导词的作用

从语法角度来看,引导同位语从句的 that 是连词,只起语法作用,用来连接同位语从句,在从句中不充当任何成分;而引导定语从句的 that 是关系代词,它除了起引导从句的语法作用之外,还要在从句中充当句子成分,主要是作主语或宾语。同位语从句的 that 一般不可以省略,但是定语从句中的关系代词如果在从句中充当宾语,在非正式用语中常常可以将关系代词 that 省略。

- The fact ***that*** he succeeded in the experiment pleased everybody.(同位语从句,that 只起连接作用)
- The fact ***that*** (***which***) we talked about is very important.(定语从句,that/which 在从句中作 about 的宾语)

3) 先行词的词性

从先行词的词性来看,同位语从句的先行词大都为抽象名词,而定语从句的先行词可以是名词,也可以是代词。

- There is no ***doubt*** that the price of wheat will go up.(同位语从句,doubt 为抽象名词)
- ***Those*** who were against the plan raised their hands.(定语从句,those 为代词)

4) 引导词与先行词的关系

who, which, what, when, why, how, where 等词都可以用来引导同位语从句,但它们的用法和用作关系代词或关系副词时引导定语从句的用法不同:引导同位语从句的关联词是对先行词的具体内容进行进一步的解释说明,与先行词不存在指代关系;而引导定语从句的关系代词或关系副词不但在从句中充当成分,而且与其修饰的先行词指代的是同一个人或者事物。

- He has solved the problem ***why*** the radio was out of order. (why 引导的是同位语从句)
- The reason ***why*** he was late for class is quite clear. (why 引导的是定语从句)

翻译:量子计算最著名的应用是破解密码,但它们最重要的应用是精确地模拟化学的量子微妙性,这个问题在制造业和工业中的用途数以千计,但传统计算机几乎完全无法解决这个问题。

11. As Moore's law runs into the sand, then, the definition of "better" will change. (Para. 24)

Paraphrase: As Moore's law gets into dilemma, people will have a different view towards what is "better".

解析:本句主要难点在于对 run into the sand 的理解,其意为 get into dilemma。

- His domestic agenda has ***run into the sand***. 其内政议程已举步维艰。

翻译:当摩尔定律陷入困境时,"更好"的定义将会改变。

12. It gave a gigantic global industry a master metronome, and a future without it will see computing progress become harder, more fitful and more irregular. (Para. 27)

Paraphrase: Moore's law sets the pace for the huge global industry. Without it, computing progress will become more difficult, less constant and less regular.

解析：metronome 的意思是指节拍器(一种在音乐演奏时能打出稳定节拍的机械，可调整至不同的速度)。因此，gave ... a master metronome 指的是 to set the pace for ...。

翻译：摩尔定律给一个庞大的全球产业设定了主要发展节奏。未来没有它，计算方面取得进步将变得更加困难，更加缺乏连续性和规律性。

写作技巧

Developing Strong Paragraphs

Overview

Body paragraphs address the main points of your argument. They divide the central idea of your paper into smaller sections and subtopics. Although each body paragraph focuses on a separate element of your main argument, paragraphs should flow together logically to create a unified essay.

➢ **Strong paragraphs should**

- ➢ relate back to your thesis statement;
- ➢ focus on only one aspect of your overall argument;
- ➢ begin with a topic sentence;
- ➢ use supporting details and examples that relate to your argument;
- ➢ end with a concluding sentence or transition smoothly into the next paragraph.

➢ **Topic Sentences**

Each body paragraph begins with a topic sentence, which conveys the paragraph's main idea. Topic sentences should not only address the scope of a particular paragraph, but also relate back to your thesis statement.

➢ **Supporting Details**

A strong paragraph should be supported by relevant details, including any specific examples, quotations, statistics, analogy, hypothetical situation that strengthen your argument. Be sure all supporting details relate back to both the topic sentence and the thesis statement.

➢ **Concluding sentences**

A strong paragraph usually ends with a concluding sentence, which restates the main idea of a paragraph.

➢ **Transitions**

Some paragraphs will conclude with a sentence that transitions into the next paragraph. A smooth transition is accomplished by relating the information in one paragraph to the topic sentence of the next paragraph.

Note that not only a paragraph can be written in this way, a section or subsection can also follow this rule to make your argument more forceful and logical. To illustrate this, we will take one section in the article as an example.

Sample Section Analysis

➢ **Sample Paragraphs**

Refer to Part 2 (Paras. 5 – 8) (contents omitted due to space limitations).

➢ **Structure Analysis**

We may first visualize the structure of this part to see how paragraphs are organized.

- **Topic sentence:**
  - But Moore's law is also a force that is nearly spent. (Para. 5)
- **Supporting paragraphs:**
  - Shrinking components gets harder. (Para. 5)
  - Business will kill Moore's law before physics does. (Paras. 6 – 7)
- **Concluding paragraph:**
  - Moore's law is near its end. (Para. 8)

In Part 1 (Paras. 1 – 4), the author focuses on the topic of the discovery of Moore's law and its influence on computing industry. In Part 2 (Paras. 5 – 8), he starts with the topic sentence "But Moore's law is also a force that is nearly spent". Note the use of transitional word "but" informs the reader of a new perspective on the main idea of the article. Then the new topic is evidenced from two perspectives, explaining why the old magic is fading. Para. 5 uses facts and data, telling us that shrinking a chip's components gets harder. Paras. 6 – 7 analyze the erosion of the financial gains due to the rising cost to make the chips. Finally, in Para. 8, the author reaches the conclusion that "Moore's law is near its end" to echo the topic sentence by citing experts' views. Following the conclusion, the next part starts with two paragraphs (Paras. 9 – 10) as a transition by relating the information in Part 2 to the topic sentence in Part 3—"There are other ways of making computers better besides shrinking their components. The end of Moore's law does not mean that the computer revolution will stall."

篇章分析

In this article, the author starts with the invention of Intel's chip 4004 in 1971 and Skylake chips in 2015. Then he compares the sizes of the two chips with analogy of the speeds of cars, indicating that this great leap from early to modern technologies is a consequence of observation of Moore's law, which noted that the number of components that could be crammed onto an integrated circuit was doubling every year. Later amended to every two years, Moore's law has become a force that sets the pace for the entire computing industry. Then, the author changes his perspective to the fact that Moore's law is near its end because shrinking a chip's components gets harder each time, and the cost to make the chips rises substantially. Despite the fading of the magic, the author points out that the end of Moore's law does not mean that the computer revolution will stall. Many technologies can be adopted to make computers faster, such as better programming, 3D chips, quantum computer, cloud computing, IoT, etc. Finally, the author gets to the conclusion that Moore's law may soon be over, but the computing revolution is not.

We visualize the text structure by means of a mind map.

Vanishing Point: The Rise of Invisible Computer

- **The great effect of Moore's law in computing industry (Paras. 1 – 4)**
  - Chip 4004—the first commercially available microprocessor in 1971 (Para. 1)
  - Skylake chips in 2015 (Para. 2)
  - A great leap from early to modern technologies (Para. 3)
  - The observation and effect of Moore's law (Para. 4)
- **But Moore's law is nearly spent. (Paras. 5 – 8)**
  - Shrinking components gets harder. (Para. 5)
  - Business will kill Moore's law. (Paras. 6 – 7)
  - Moore's law is near its end. (Para. 8)
- **Other ways to make computers better (Paras. 9 – 26)**
  - Transition: The computer revolution will not stall. (Paras. 9 – 10)
  - Other ways to make computers faster (Paras. 11 – 26)
    - Better programming (Para. 11)
    - Chips with specialized circuitry (Para. 12)
    - 3D chips (Paras. 13 – 15)
    - Quantum computing(Paras. 16 – 18)
    - Cloud computing (Paras. 19 – 21)
    - IoT (Paras. 22 – 23)
    - Other possible ways (Paras. 24 – 26)
- **Conclusion: Moore's law may soon be over. The computing revolution is not. (Para. 27)**

课堂提问

- What do you know about computing science, cloud computing, quantum computing and IoT?
- What are the strengths and weaknesses of computers?

教学建议

This article introduces the observation and effect of Moore's law on computing industry, and the future technological development in the industry. The sentence structures involved are not too difficult, but students need to analyze and understand some phrases and sentences. Therefore, students are well advised to conduct an intensive reading of the article. Meanwhile, the article is well organized. By analyzing its structure and writing skills, students will learn how to write strong paragraphs.

B. 课堂讨论模块

学习时间

2 hours

讨论内容

- Are we becoming too reliant on computers? Will we be made redundant by our machines?
- Do you know any technologies that play key roles in the development of computers?
- Use your professional knowledge to predict the future of computer.

教学方法

heuristic teaching; group discussion; class presentation

组织形式

- Let students as groups present a PPT about computing science.
- Discuss in groups their expectation of the future computer and then present their group's idea after discussion.

参考问题

- Do you know the whole development of computer?
- What are the benefits and troubles that computer brings us?
- What do you think is the future of computer?

课后练习

Refer to the exercises in Unit One of the textbook.

练习答案

Part 1　Reading Comprehension

1. Directions: Do the following statements agree with the information given in the reading passage? In blanks 1)-5), choose

TRUE　　　　　　　if the statement agrees with the information.
FALSE　　　　　　 if the statement contradicts the information.
NOT GIVEN　　　　 if there is no such information in the statement.

1) F (Para.3)　2) NG (Para.5)　3) T (Para.11)　4) F (Para.16)　5) T (Para.25)

2. Directions: Paraphrase the following sentences.

1) Moore's law almost exerts its full potential. It may soon be over.
2) Moore's law will soon come to an end. People propose an assumption that computers will get better and cheaper at high speed in the future.
3) There are some easy methods to make computers faster and cheaper.
4) As Moore's law gets into dilemma, people will have a different view towards "better".
5) Moore's law sets the pace for the entire computing industry.

Part 2　Words and Expressions

3. Directions: Choose proper words from the following word bank, and fill in blanks in their right forms.

1) feature　2) conceivable　3) incentive　4) boost　5) erosion
6) exotic　7) obscurity　8) consensus　9) sluggish　10) revenue

Part 3　Translation

4. Directions: Translate the following sentences from the reading passage into Chinese.

1) 这块芯片是这个时代的奇迹，由 2 300 个微小的晶体管构成，每个晶体管直径大约 10 000 纳米(或十亿分之一米)，大约相当于一个红细胞的大小。晶体管是一种电子开关，通过在“开”和“关”之间的切换，从物理层面上表示基本信息元 1 和 0。
2) 每个晶体管之间间隔 14 纳米，体积非常小，肉眼不可见，因为它们比人类能够看到的光的波长小一个数量级。
3) 每次缩小芯片元件都会变得愈加困难，并且因为现代晶体管只有几十个原子大小，工程师们完全没有改进的空间。
4) 然而，商业将先于物理学扼杀摩尔定律，因为压缩晶体管无法带来之前那样大的收益。被称为“登纳德缩放比例定律”的相关发现(以 1974 年首次正式提出该想法的 IBM 工程师 Robert Dennard 的名字命名)使摩尔定律如虎添翼，这个定律指出缩小芯片组件会使芯片速度更快、耗电更少且生产成本更低。
5) 例如，自动驾驶汽车将越来越多地利用机器视觉，其中，计算机学会解析来自现实世界的图像，把目标分类，并且提取信息，这种任务对计算要求相当之高。

Part 4　Sentence Structure

5. Directions: Combine the following sentences in each group into a complex sentence.

1) At the same time these computers record which hours are busiest and which employers are the most efficient, allowing personnel and staffing assignments to be made accordingly.
2) In the American economy, the concept of private property embraces not only the

ownership of productive resources but also certain rights, including the right to determine the price of a product or to make a free contract with another private individual.

3) If, on the other hand, producing more of a commodity results in reducing its cost, this will tend to increase the supply offered by seller-producers, which in turn will lower the price and permit more consumers to buy the product.

4) Thus, in the American economic system, it is the demand of individual consumers, coupled with the desire of businessmen to maximize profits and the desire of individuals to maximize their incomes, that together determines what shall be produced and how resources are used to produce it.

5) The great interest in exceptional children shown in public education over the past three decades indicates the strong feeling in our society that all citizens, whatever their special conditions, deserve the opportunity to fully develop their capabilities.

Part 5 Academic Writing Skills

6. Directions: Choose a verb from the word bank to replace each italicized expression. Note that you may need to add tense to the verb from the bank. Write down any other single verbs that you think could also work in the sentences.

1) tolerate 2) investigating 3) determine 4) developed 5) constitute

6) eliminate 7) reached 8) maintain 9) decreased 10) considering

7. Directions: Write a few single verbs that could be used in place of the italicized expressions. In each case, try to find two or three possibilities and be prepared to discuss them.

1) encountered 2) raised/posed/introduced 3) emerged/arose/occurred

4) designed/developed/proposed/presented/built/constructed 5) checked/examined

8. Directions: Decide which of the italicized expressions are more suitable for an academic paper.

1) an integral part of 2) nearly 3) considerable 4) robust 5) increasing

Unit Two
Wireless Communication Technology

Section A The Race for 5G: Why China Wants to Lead Next Generation Wireless Internet

文章主旨

This text, by exploring in depth historical lessons and IPRs consideration, tells us China's ambition to lead the global 5G race. Though, the country and its companies are encountering strong opposition from the west. There is no clear signal as to who will win the 5G race eventually and how.

教学目标

- To learn the global 5G competitive landscape, China's position and the stories behind.
- To master the technical words and expressions related to 5G technology.
- To be able to use the knowledge learned to discuss issues about the 5G race.

学习时间

4 hours (2 hours for the text; 2 hours for discussion)

A. 课堂讲授模块

预习要求

- To learn and recite the new words.
- To grasp the main idea of the text after reading.
- To search for materials related to 5G technology and competition.

学习时间

2 hours

教学方法

heuristic teaching; project-based teaching; task-driven teaching; group discussion; self-study and peer learning

组织形式

- Let the students work in groups to discuss the structure and main idea of the text based on fast reading, and to draw a simple mind-map as well.
- Summarize key technical terms, words and phrases, and sentence patterns in the article involving 5G, Made in China 2025, 3G standards, intellectual property rights, working frequency, etc.
- Let students discuss in groups the gains based on their fields of research, and a presentation is expected.
- Analyze the complex sentences and technical issues. Spare some time to respond to any questions from students.

背景知识

1. International Telecommunication Union

The International Telecommunication Union (ITU) (国际电信联盟) is an agency of the United Nations (UN) whose purpose is to coordinate telecommunication operations and services throughout the world. Originally founded in 1865, as the International Telegraph Union, the ITU is the oldest existing international organization. ITU headquarters are in Geneva, Switzerland.

The ITU consists of three sectors:

- Radiocommunication (ITU-R)—ensures optimal, fair and rational use of the radio frequency (RF) spectrum
- Telecommunication Standardization (ITU-T)—formulates recommendations for standardizing telecommunication operations worldwide
- Telecommunication Development (ITU-D)—assists countries in developing and maintaining internal communication operations

The ITU sets and publishes regulations and standards relevant to electronic communication and broadcasting technologies of all kinds including radio, television, satellite, telephone and the Internet. The organization conducts working parties, study groups and meetings to address current and future issues and to resolve disputes. The ITU organizes and holds an exhibition and forum known as the Global TELECOM every four years.

2. Qualcomm

Qualcomm Incorporated (美国高通公司) is an American multinational semiconductor and telecommunications equipment company that designs and markets wireless telecommunications products and services. It derives most of its revenue from chipmaking and the bulk of its profit from patent licensing businesses. The company is headquartered in San Diego, California, United States, and has 224 locations worldwide.

The parent company is Qualcomm Incorporated (Qualcomm), which has a number of wholly owned subsidiaries: Qualcomm CDMA Technologies (QCT) sells all of Qualcomm's products and services (including chipsets); Qualcomm Technology Licensing (QTL) is responsible for the patent licensing businesses; and Qualcomm Technologies, Inc. (QTI) operates nearly all of Qualcomm's R&D activities.

3. GlobalData Plc

GlobalData Plc is a data analytics and consulting company that was established in 1999, and has been listed on the London Stock Exchange (伦敦证券交易所) since 2000. It was previously called Progressive Digital Media and before that, the TMN Group. Its corporate headquarters is in London, and it also has offices across the UK, U. S., Argentina, South Korea, Mexico, China, Japan, India and Australia. The group is chaired by Bernard Cragg, former finance director of Carlton TV, and the company founder, Mike Danson, is CEO. Danson was also one of the founders of Datamonitor.

4. Counterpoint Technology Market Research

Counterpoint Technology Market Research is a global research firm specializing in mobile & technology products in the TMT industry. Headquartered in Hong Kong of China, it has teams based in key industry centers: Seoul, South Korea; Gurgaon and Mumbai, India; London, UK; San Diego, U. S.; Beijing, China; and Buenos Aires, Argentina. It services major technology firms and financial firms with a mix of monthly reports, customized projects and detailed analysis of the mobile and technology markets.

5. Jefferies Financial Group

Jefferies is a diversified financial services company engaged in investment banking and capital markets, asset management and direct investing. Jefferies Group offers a full range of investment banking, equities, fixed income, asset and wealth management products and services. The company was founded in 1968 and is headquartered in New York, NY.

6. Made in China 2025

"Made in China 2025" (中国制造 2025) is a national plan authorized by Premier Li Keqiang in 2015 seeking to modernize China's manufacturing by encouraging innovation and use of high technology. It is the first 10-year action plan, followed by another two plans, designed to transform China from a manufacturing giant into a world manufacturing power by the year 2049, which will be the 100th anniversary of the founding of the People's Republic of China.

In the plan, nine tasks have been identified as priorities: improving manufacturing innovation, integrating information technology and industry, strengthening the industrial base, fostering Chinese brands, enforcing green manufacturing, promoting breakthroughs in 10 key sectors, advancing restructuring of the manufacturing sector, promoting service-oriented manufacturing and manufacturing-related service industries, and internationalizing manufacturing.

The 10 key sectors are new information technology, numerical control tools and robotics, aerospace equipment, ocean engineering equipment and high-tech ships, railway equipment, energy saving and new energy vehicles, power equipment, new materials, biological medicine and medical devices, and agricultural machinery.

7. The 3rd Generation Partnership Project

The 3rd Generation Partnership Project (3GPP) is a collaboration between groups of telecommunications associations (ARIB, ATIS, CCSA, ETSI, TSDSI, TTA, TTC), known as the Organizational Partners, and provides their members with a stable environment to produce the Reports and Specifications that define 3GPP technologies.

The project covers cellular telecommunications network technologies, including radio access, the core transport network, and service capabilities—including work on codecs (编解码器), security, quality of service—and thus provides complete system specifications. The specifications also provide hooks for non-radio access to the core network, and for interworking with Wi-Fi networks.

8. Federal Communications Commission

The Federal Communications Commission (FCC) (美国联邦通信委员会) is an independent government agency responsible for regulating the radio, television and phone industries. The FCC regulates interstate and international communications by radio, television, wire, satellite, and cable in all 50 states, the District of Columbia and U.S. territories. An independent U.S. government agency overseen by Congress, the Commission is the federal agency responsible for implementing and enforcing America's communications law and regulations.

The FCC's key responsibilities range from issuing operating licenses for radio and TV stations to maintaining decency standards designed to protect the public good. The commission is led by a five-member partisan board consisting of Republican and Democratic nominees selected by the President.

9. Frost & Sullivan

Frost & Sullivan, the Growth Partnership Company, enables clients to accelerate growth and achieve best in growth, innovation and leadership. The company's Growth Partnership Service provides the CEO and the CEO's Growth Team with disciplined research and best practice models to drive the generation, evaluation and implementation of powerful growth strategies.

Frost & Sullivan was founded in 1961 in New York City with a specific mission: To publish world-class market consulting information and intelligence on emerging high-technology and industrial markets. The company soon developed a reputation as one of the world's leading companies in growth consulting and corporate training. Now well into its fourth decade, Frost & Sullivan has won a worldwide reputation for publishing high-quality growth consulting and training reports in more than 20 major industries.

重点词汇

1. **chauffeur** /ˈʃəʊfə(r)/ *n*. a person whose job is to drive a car, especially for somebody rich or important（尤指富人或要人的）司机；*v*. to drive somebody in a car, usually as your job 为(某人)开车，当……司机
   - Imagine a city of the future, a city where commuters are ***chauffeured*** to work by self-driving cars and where artificial intelligence systems control every power plant, traffic light and light bulb, making road accidents, power cuts and even traffic jams a thing of the past. (Para. 1)
   - Thirty-year-old Ravinder Pande works as a ***chauffeur*** for a businessman in New Delhi earning $200 a month.
   - He had also survived multiple assassination attempts in the past, including a 1994 car bomb that decapitated his ***chauffeur***.
2. **protocol** /ˈprəʊtəkɒl/ *n*. 1) a system of rules about the correct way to act in formal situations 礼节；2) a set of rules for exchanging information between computers（计算机间交换信息的）协议
   - Thanks to 5G, the latest ***protocol*** for mobile communications, this vision may be realized much sooner than you think. (Para. 2)
   - He has become a stickler for the finer observances of diplomatic visits ***protocol***.
3. **vista** /ˈvɪstə/ *n*. 1) a beautiful view, for example, of the countryside, a city, etc.（农村、城市等的）景色，景观；2) a range of things that might happen in the future（未来可能发生的）一系列情景，一连串事情
   - This will open a ***vista*** of new technological possibilities. (Para. 3)
   - Finally, on a glorious day the summit is reached, the mountain is tamed and a magnificent ***vista*** is opened up.
   - These uprisings come from desperation and a ***vista*** of a future without hope.
4. **seamless** /ˈsiːmləs/ *adj*. 1) without a seam 无(接)缝的；2) with no spaces or pauses between one part and the next(两部分之间)无空隙的，不停顿的
   - The gains in network speed and reliability will enable billions of internet-enabled devices to connect and coordinate themselves ***seamlessly*** in real time. (Para. 4)
   - From what we're hearing, HP wants to create a ***seamless*** experience for all of their hardware.
   - The projected images are aligned such that they form a nearly ***seamless*** image on the projection screen.
5. **supremacy** /sjuːˈpreməsi/ *n*. a position in which you have more power, authority or

status than anyone else 至高无上,最大权力,最高权威,最高地位

➢ Like the transitions to 3G and 4G, the battle for 5G ***supremacy*** is being fought mainly by the leading telecom players including European companies Ericsson and Nokia, Samsung of South Korea and the U.S.'s Qualcomm. (Para. 7)

➢ The great object of all social teaching should be to promote the ***supremacy*** of altruism over egoism.

➢ Even more than the Japanese victories in the second world war, it announced the end of white ***supremacy*** over the continent and the beginning of the rise of the East.

6. also-ran /ˈɔːlsəʊ ræn/ *n*. a person who is not successful, especially in a competition or an election 失败者,(尤指竞赛或竞选的)失利者

➢ China's telecom firms were little more than ***also-rans*** during the transitions to 3G and 4G—and paid the price for it. (Para. 8)

➢ Yahoo!'s status as the ***also-ran*** that seemed poised to inherit the internet, but failed to keep up with the changing technological times, is cemented.

7. leverage /ˈliːvərɪdʒ/ *n*. 1) the ability to influence situations or people so that you can control what happens 影响力; 2) the act of using a lever to open or lift something; the force used to do this 杠杆作用,杠杆效力; *v*. 1) to use borrowed capital for (an investment), expecting the profits made to be greater than the interest payable 举债经营; 2) to use (something) to maximum advantage 最大限度地利用,最优化使用

➢ It is crucial that Chinese companies ***leverage*** China's pole position in the 5G race to shape the global standards. (Para. 17)

➢ If you can understand that debt can be good, and carefully learn to use debt as ***leverage***, you will gain an advantage over most savers.

➢ A benevolent explanation is that it has ***leverage*** over its ally, Armenia.

➢ He might feel that ***leveraging*** the company at a time when he sees tremendous growth opportunities would be a mistake.

8. overhaul /ˈəʊvəhɔːl/ *n*. an examination of a machine or system, including doing repairs on it or making changes to it 检修,大修,改造; *v*. to examine every part of a machine, system, etc. and make any necessary changes or repairs 彻底检修

➢ According to Rogers, equipment vendors, by working with partners can ensure that their early investments in trial 5G equipment will be able to be deployed without any major ***overhaul*** once 5G has been fully standardized. (Para. 20)

➢ But banks are reluctant to ***overhaul*** this legacy software owing to the cost and complexity involved.

➢ The district, the nation's second largest, agreed to a complete ***overhaul*** of its English-learning program.

9. **shun** /ʃʌn/ *v*. to avoid somebody/something 避开，回避，避免

➢ In the 2000s, when the rest of the world started to move onto 3G, which allowed mobile users access to the internet, China decided that it would ***shun*** dependence on Western technology. (Para. 25)

➢ She was ***shunned*** by her family when she remarried.

10. **broker** /ˈbrəʊkə(r)/ *n*. a person who buys and sells things for other people 经纪人，掮客；*v*. to arrange the details of an agreement, especially between different countries 安排，协商(协议的细节，尤指在两国间)

➢ The battlefield on which this regulatory fight will play out is a task force under the ITU called the third Generation Partnership Project (3GPP), which is meant to ***broker*** agreements on what performance requirements 5G will have to achieve. (Para. 32)

➢ However, with the ***broker's*** knowledge of investment, finance, and value, and the consumer's quandary over where to invest, you have an opportunity.

11. **gnash** /næʃ/ *v*. to feel very angry and upset about something, especially because you cannot get what you want(气得)咬牙切齿

➢ The decision was hailed throughout China as proof that the country is a contender in the race to define and develop 5G, but set teeth ***gnashing*** in the U.S. (Para. 34)

➢ It makes me ***gnash*** my teeth to see so much food deliberately destroyed or wasted when there are people starving in Africa.

12. **furlong** /ˈfɜːlɒŋ/ *n*. A furlong is a unit of length that is equal to 220 yards or 201.2 meters. 弗隆，浪(长度单位，等于 220 码或 201.2 米)

➢ With the race for 5G entering the final ***furlong***, the eventual outcome still looks far from clear. (Para. 40)

➢ "Although he was beaten in his first race at seven ***furlongs***, I was thrilled with his performance." the trainer said.

13. **tilt** /tɪlt/ *v*. 1) to move, or make something move, into a position with one side or end higher than the other(使)倾斜，倾侧；2) If a person or thing tilts toward a particular opinion or if something tilts them toward it, they change slightly so that they become more in agreement with that opinion or position. 倾向

➢ The 5G world may not run on Chinese rules, but there is no doubt that the balance of power is ***tilting*** eastward. (Para. 44)

➢ To generate lift, a bird has merely to ***tilt*** its wings, adjusting the flow of air below and above them.

➢ Lisbon would ***tilt*** the balance of power a bit toward Luxembourg, but not as far as its opponents fear.

重点短语

1. **roll out**: If a company rolls out a new product or service, or if the product or service rolls out, it is made available to the public. 推出(新产品或服务)
   - ➢ The world's leading telecom companies are already testing the next generation of wireless internet and the first 5G services could ***be rolled out*** as early as 2019. (Para. 2)
   - ➢ Northern Telecom says its products will ***roll out*** over 18 months beginning early next year.
   - ➢ When an application is compromised, you also need an elegant way to ***roll out*** replacement API keys.
2. **reckon with**: If you say that there is someone or something to be reckoned with, you mean that they must be dealt with and it will be difficult. 认真处理,小心对付
   - ➢ But this time, China's Huawei and ZTE have also emerged as forces to ***be reckoned with***. (Para. 7)
   - ➢ Whether Abenomics succeeds or fails, Japan's government must ultimately ***reckon with*** its years of deficit spending and mountainous debt.
   - ➢ However hard companies try to pay staff in different countries the same way, they still have to ***reckon with*** different taxes and benefits.
3. **at stake**: If something is at stake, it is being risked and might be lost or damaged if you are not successful. 处于危险境地,处于成败关头
   - ➢ A recent report by the China Academy of Information and Communication Technology (CAICT) made clear what is ***at stake*** for China. (Para. 11)
   - ➢ When you're older you've got a lot more ***at stake*** and want to be more conservative.
   - ➢ From the way she acted, he knew there was something more serious ***at stake*** than just the physical damage from an automobile accident.
4. **ahead of the pack**: more successful than your competitors or rivals(在竞赛中)领先其他对手
   - ➢ The Chinese government's planning is starting to pay off, as China nudges ***ahead of the pack*** to make the 5G world a reality. (Para. 13)
   - ➢ This new management system has kept the company far ***ahead of the pack*** in terms of product development.
   - ➢ While it's virtually impossible to pinpoint the most cell phone producer in the world, it's easy to tell which companies are ***ahead of the pack***.
5. **scale up**: If you scale up something, you make it greater in size, amount, or extent than it used to be. 增加,放大
   - ➢ The Chinese, in turn, try to push for 5G at medium frequency and ***scale up*** the

industry in order to reduce the cost. (Para. 31)

➤ But companies cannot readily ***scale up*** the process from the 400 million doses of regular flu vaccine they make each year to the billions needed in a pandemic.

6. **in the wake of**: following directly or close behind; following as a consequence 随着，紧紧跟随

➤ The U.S. Federal Communications Commission (FCC), which can barely hide its deep dissatisfaction with the 3GPP's standard-setting process, put out a terse statement ***in the wake of*** the decision. (Para. 35)

➤ Markets seem to have realized that their pessimism ***in the wake of*** the Japanese earthquake was overdone and have recovered some ground.

7. **give somebody a run for one's money**: to not allow someone to win easily 不让……轻易取胜，与……进行激烈竞争

➤ There they are ***giving Ericsson and Nokia a run for their money*** on their home turf, according to Neil Wang, Greater China president of researchers Frost & Sullivan. (Para. 37)

➤ Our motorcycle company has enjoyed being the industry leader, but lately one of our rivals has been ***giving us a run for our money***.

8. **pale into insignificance**: to seem not important when compared with something else 相比之下微不足道，黯然失色

➤ ... this ***pales into insignificance*** compared to the massive amount of collaboration occurring between Japan, South Korea and the U.S. ... (Para. 39)

➤ But when compared with the amount that China either produces or consumes today, those numbers ***pale into insignificance***.

9. **dig one's heels in**: to refuse stubbornly to move or be persuaded 固执己见；采取坚定的立场

➤ The U.S. government currently appears to be ***digging its heels in***, as the FCC has already allocated super high frequency for 5G. (Para. 42)

➤ Well, I've already told Grace that she couldn't go. But she seemed to ***dig her heels in*** as if the party was the most important thing in her life.

难句解析

1. With key emerging industries like the Internet of Things (IoT), virtual reality and autonomous vehicles all relying on the rollout of 5G, the countries and operators that take the lead in mastering and deploying these next-generation networks are likely to gain significant financial and competitive advantages. (Para. 6)

Paraphrase: As new industries like IoT, virtual reality and autonomous vehicles depend on the development of 5G, the countries and operators who are among the first to master and apply these new technologies have more chances of winning over others in terms of finance.

解析：全句的主干是 the countries and operators are likely to gain advantages，that 引导的定语从句进一步修饰主语，说明是哪些国家和运营商有可能获得巨大经济和竞争优势，而句首的"with＋宾语＋现在分词（宾补）"作原因状语修饰主句，强调原因"物联网、虚拟现实和无人驾驶等重点新兴行业均依赖于 5G 的上线"。"with＋宾语＋宾补"的复合结构，主要有以下几种形式：

➢ "with＋宾语＋形容词（宾补）"在句中作状语：Unlike his roommates，he likes to sleep with the window open in the dorm.

➢ "with＋宾语＋副词（宾补）"在句中作状语：With her son away from home，she was worried.

➢ "with＋宾语＋介词短语（宾补）"在句中作状语：She came in with a baby in her arms，humming a cradlesong gently.

➢ "with＋宾语＋现在分词（宾补）"在句中作状语：With a local guide leading the way，we found the village easily.

➢ "with＋宾语＋过去分词（宾补）"在句中作状语：With the problem solved，we went on to consider other technical issues in the system.

➢ "with＋宾语＋不定式（宾补）"在句中作状语：With the best doctor to help her，she believed that she could recover fully.

➢ "with＋宾语＋介词短语（宾补）"在句中作定语：The lady with a purse in her hand was one of the best-known public speakers in the country.

翻译：诸如物联网、虚拟现实和无人驾驶等重点新兴行业均依赖于 5G 的面世，因而掌握并部署下一代 5G 网络的国家及运营商就有可能获得巨大的经济和竞争优势。

2. Making China the global leader in 5G is also one of the cornerstones of "Made in China 2025"，the ambitious industrial strategy launched by the Chinese government in 2015 that aims to make the country the world's leading high-tech manufacturing power. (Para. 10)

Paraphrase：Chinese government introduced in 2015 "Made in China 2025" industrial strategy，the ambition of which is to make China lead the world in high-tech manufacturing. To lay a foundation for this aim，China must become a global leader in 5G.

解析：此句的主句比较简单，主语是动名词短语 Making China the global leader in 5G，谓语紧随其后 is also one of the cornerstones of ....。句子之所以长，是因为修饰"Made in China 2025"的同位语 the ambitious industrial strategy 后面又接了两个后置定语，一个是过去分词短语 launched by the Chinese government in 2015，另一个是 that 引导的定语从句。

翻译：中国政府 2015 年雄心勃勃地推出了"中国制造 2025"产业战略计划，旨在使其成为全球领先的高科技制造强国。而实现该计划的重要支撑之一便是领跑 5G 发展。

3. Huawei and ZTE，already well positioned to become major global players in 5G due to the wide adoption of their mobile equipment across Asia and Europe, have also shocked their rivals by the speed at which they have developed new network technology. (Para. 14)

Paraphrase: Mobile equipment by Huawei and ZTE is widely used in Asia and Europe. As a result, they are fully ready to take part in the global 5G race and have shocked their rivals because they have developed new network technology at a high rate.

解析：此句理解上的难点在于主句 Huawei and ZTE ... have also shocked their rivals ... 被过去分词短语 positioned to 隔开，其作用相当于主语的后置定语。句子长是因为修饰语较多，due to ... 作状语来解释华为、中兴两家制造商为什么能准备就绪参加 5G 竞跑，at which 引导的定语从句修饰 speed。

翻译：华为和中兴的移动设备在亚欧广泛使用，因而它们都已准备就绪参加 5G 全球之争。而且，这两家厂商开发网络新技术速度之快，令其竞争对手都震撼不已。

4. Whereas China is enthusiastic about the medium frequency, which offers wide coverage, the U.S. supports the super high frequency. (Para. 29)

Paraphrase: China would like to build 5G on medium frequency for wide coverage. However, the U.S. is in favor of super high frequency.

解析：此句主要理解 whereas 的用法。whereas 主要用来比较或对比两个事实，其意为"然而，但是，尽管"，既可以放在句首，也可以放在句中。举例如下：

➢ ***Whereas*** the population of working age increased by 1 million between 1981 and 1986, today it is barely growing.

➢ First of all, programmers tend to do technically impressive things ***whereas*** the most successful social software rather "starts out doing one task supremely well".

翻译：中国对覆盖范围更广的中频青睐不已，而美国则支持超高频。

5. Each working group will come up with engineering solutions for each component backed up with trial data in order to reach consensus as to which proposal is the best. (Para. 33)

Paraphrase: For each component, to agree on the best proposal, each working group will present its engineering solutions supported by trial data.

解析：本句虽不长，但结构较为复杂。主干部分是 Each working group will come up with engineering solutions，宾语 solutions 后面接了两个后置定语，一个是介词短语 for each component，一个是过去分词短语 backed up with。in order to 引导目的状语修饰主句，as to+宾语从句整体充当 consensus 的定语。

翻译：为了就最佳提议达成一致，所有工作组都要提出针对每一部件、由实验数据支撑的工程解决方案。

6. Given that the availability of free spectrum is a very big factor for telecom operators, Lee believes that a compromise may be reached, in which the world settles for medium-to-low frequency with super high frequency being used as a supplement in densely-populated city centers. (Para. 43)

Paraphrase: For telecom operators, whether free spectrum can be used is a big concern. Lee believes that both sides need to take one step back, reaching an agreement that medium-to-low frequency dominates most of the world whereas super high frequency will aid to play its part in city centers with a lot of population.

解析：本句主干部分 Lee believes 很简单，难点在于 Given that 引导的原因状语从句，以及其后 in which 引导的定语从句。而在定语从句中，又有"with＋宾语＋过去分词（宾补）"结构作状语。

翻译：对电信运营商来说，自由频谱的可用性绝对是重中之重。因此，李相信最终双方会各退一步，即中到低频成为主流，而超高频则在人口稠密的城市中心作为补充。

写作技巧

Constructing Supporting Evidence

Overview

After identifying the main point that you want to make about a topic, the central claim of your essay, what counts as effective supporting evidence for this claim? Normally, supporting evidence consists of facts, statistics, authoritative opinions, quotable comments, anecdotes, clarifying examples. They could be used separately or in combination, depending on your purpose and audience.

➢ **Facts**

The most frequently used type of evidence in an essay is facts. Facts include names, dates, or specific events. In literature, evidence takes the form of plot summaries or specific quotations.

➢ **Statistics**

Statistics convey information in numerical form. Statistics are most accessible and convincing when they are used sparingly and in combination with an explanation as to why the numbers are significant. Remember that even though statistics are considered factual, numbers can be presented in different ways to suggest dramatically different conclusions. Pay attention to any conflicting information you find and be sure to provide the full context of statistical data.

➢ **Authoritative Opinions**

Expert opinions are based on factual evidence but differ from facts in that they are interpretations of them. Expert opinions may not be as reliable as facts or personal experience, but they are a useful and common means of supporting an argument. In much of the argumentative writing you do, you will rely upon the opinions of experts in the field you are studying both to determine your own perspective and to support your claims.

➢ **Quotable Comments**

Quotable comments provide support for your argument but should not be overused. Be sure the quote emanates from an authoritative source and is not misleading.

➢ **Anecdotes**

Anecdotes are humorous experiences that illustrate your point. In addition to supporting your argument, anecdotes can liven up an otherwise boring academic paper.

➢ **Clarifying Examples**

Examples that clarify your points and support your thesis statement make great evidence. Appropriate examples can support the writer's contention that a general statement is true. Not only do they provide specifics and details in support of a claim, but the vivid description they often include helps to capture and retain readers' attention.

Sample Section Analysis

➢ **Sample Paragraphs**

Refer to Paras. 8 - 16 (contents omitted due to space limitations).

➢ **Structure Analysis**

We may first visualize the structure of this part to see how paragraphs are organized.

- **Topic:**
  - China's 5G Dream (as suggested by the subtitle)
- **Supporting paragraphs:**
  - China's determined not to repeat its past failure in 5G race. (Para. 8)
  - China's been planning and preparing from policy support, telecom groups' investment, etc. (Paras. 9 - 12)
  - China's move gets paid off. (Paras. 13 - 16)

As the subtitle well suggests, the central claim of this section is China's 5G dream. After reviewing briefly the fact that China's telecom firms were little more than also-rans during the transitions to 3G and 4G, it points out that both they and the Chinese government are determined not to let this happen again (Para. 8). The claim is evidenced from several perspectives. First, several facts concerning government policy support are provided, including the founding of the IMT-2020(5G) Promotion Group (Para. 9), the launch of "Made in China 2025" (Para. 10), etc. Then, exact figures and data are quoted to show the potential economic output of "RMB 6.3 trillion ($947 billion) by 2030" driven by 5G developing, (Para. 11), and a vast investment of "RMB 2.8 trillion ($420 billion) between 2020 and 2030" from China's telecom groups (Para. 12). All these facts and numbers suggest China has spared no effort to fulfill its 5G dream. Last, an example is used to prove how fast and how well China's telecom giants are developing new network technology, the demonstration of a new device combining several key 5G technologies by Huawei at PT Expo China 2017 (Para. 14). Reports and comments by German online publication teltarif. de is quoted as further demonstration that "... they are ready for the next generation of mobile telecom, not only in theory, but also in practice." (Paras. 15 – 16), supporting in a very powerful way the claim: "China's 5G dream".

篇章分析

In this article, the author starts with a vision of the future city converging 5G technology in all walks of life, followed by a description of functions and conveniences brought by 5G. Then a smooth turn is made to introduce the 5G battle fought among the global telecom players since it is viewed as a game-changer for businesses and governments. In "China's 5G Dream", facts, figures and quotes are made to show what efforts Chinese government and enterprises have made in the 5G race and how they work out. Furthermore, the article points out in "Setting New Standards" the vital importance for China to shape the global 5G standards, as this concerns cutting cost, building partnership, reducing time to market, and getting intellectual property rights (IRRs). After reviewing briefly in "Fifth Time Lucky" the history of transitions to 1G, 2G, 3G and 4G, particularly the bitter experience of Chinese players, the article turns to discuss in "What's the Frequency?" and "Western Headwinds" the strong opposition from the West to China's ambition in leading 5G development. One fierce competition is that China is enthusiastic about the medium frequency offering wide coverage, while the U.S. supports the super high frequency. Besides, both Huawei and ZTE are at a risk of being shut out from the Western countries due to their lack of close partners within the industry. Though, based on analyzing and reasoning, it admits in the last section "Unclear signals" that the 5G world may not run on Chinese rules, the balance of power is tilting eastward.

We visualize the text structure by means of a mind map.

The Race for 5G

- **The Future 5G Cities (Paras. 1 – 7)**
  - Vision of future 5G cities (Para. 1)
  - Functions of 5G (Paras. 2 – 5)
  - Battle for 5G supremacy (Paras. 6 – 7)
- **China's 5G Dream (Paras. 8 – 16)**
  - China's determination (Para. 8)
  - Policy support from government (Paras. 9 – 11)
  - Investment plan by telecom groups(Para. 12)
  - Planning starting to pay off (Paras. 13 – 16)

- **Setting New Standards (Paras. 17 – 23)**
  - Vital importance of sharing global 5G standards (Paras. 17 – 20)
  - Another reason: IPRs(Paras. 21 – 23)
- **Fifth Time Lucky (Paras. 24 – 28)**
  - History of transitions to 2G, 3G and 4G (Paras. 24 – 26)
  - Seizing opportunities in 5G transition (Paras. 27 – 28)
- **What's the Frequency? (Paras. 29 – 35)**
  - Frequency battle between China and U.S. (Paras. 29 – 31)
  - China's early victory in 3GPP (Paras. 32 – 35)
- **Western Headwinds (Paras. 36 – 39)**
  - Huawei and ZTE banned from American market (Para. 36)
  - Lack of close partnerships in other key markets (Paras. 37 – 39)
- **Unclear Signals (Paras. 40 – 44)**
  - The outcome of the battle still unclear (Paras. 40 – 42)
  - A compromise likely to be reached (Paras. 43 – 44)

课堂提问

- What do you know about history of wireless communication?
- What are the applications of 5G technology?

教学建议

This article introduces China's 5G dream and its position in the global 5G competitive landscape. The sentence structures involved are not very difficult, but there are some technical words and phrases for students to understand. Besides, the students must also refer to the history of wireless communication technology to better grasp the ideas between the lines. Therefore, students are well advised to conduct an intensive reading of the article. Meanwhile, the article is well organized, as there are subtitles summarizing the main idea of each section. By analyzing its structure and writing skills, students will learn how to construct supporting evidences for a claim they make.

B. 课堂讨论模块

学习时间

2 hours

讨论内容

- In what aspects is 5G different from the last generation of wireless communication technology and how is it going to change people's life?

- What do you think are the major reasons for China's determination to become the global leader in 5G?
- Compare technically the global telecom giants like Huawei, Qualcomm and Ericsson concerning their positions in the 5G competitive landscape.

教学方法

heuristic teaching; group discussion; class presentation

组织形式

- Let students in groups present a PPT about 5G technology.
- Discuss in groups their understanding of the global 5G competitive landscape and the challenges faced by China, and then present their group's idea after discussion.

参考问题

- Do you know the development history of wireless communication technology?
- What are the possible application scenarios of 5G?
- Who do you think will win the 5G competition?

课后练习

Refer to the exercises in Unit Two of the text book.

练习答案

Part 1 Reading Comprehension

1. Directions: The reading passage has 49 paragraphs. Which paragraph contains the following information? Write the correct number, 1 - 49, in blanks 1)- 5).

1) Para. 42 2) Para. 10 3) Para. 29 4) Para. 18 5) Para. 26

2. Directions: Paraphrase the following sentences.

1) But this time, China's Huawei and ZTE are becoming forces that cannot be ignored.

2) In a recent report, China Academy of Information and Communication Technology (CAICT) clearly stated the importance of 5G for China.

3) We can understand why China invest large sum of money on the development of telecom when we consider the fact that China has a very large internal market.

4) With China gradually taking the lead in the race for 5G, Chinese government's plan of Made in China 2025 is beginning to bear fruit.

5) The decision was welcomed in China because it proved that the country is a contestant in the race to define and develop 5G, but the U. S. was rather dissatisfied with the result.

Part 2 Words and Expressions

3. Directions: Choose proper words from the following word bank, and fill in blanks in their right forms.

1) was enthusiastic about 2) in the wake of 3) is aligned with 4) roll out
5) in terms of 6) be vulnerable to 7) be reckoned with 8) settle for
9) other than 10) at stake

Part 3 Translation

4. Directions: Translate the following sentences from the reading passage into Chinese.

1) 想象一下未来的城市，在这个城市里，通勤者驾驶自动驾驶汽车去上班，人工智能系统控制着每一个电厂、交通信号灯和灯泡，交通事故、停电甚至交通堵塞都成为过去。

2) 网络速度和可靠性的提高将使数十亿具有互联网功能的设备能够实现实时无缝连接和协调。在道路上，自动驾驶汽车将能够感知彼此的移动，并调整速度和方向以避免碰撞。

3) 为了应对这种情况，两家公司都将重点放在了澳大利亚、印度、日本、拉丁美洲和欧盟等其他关键市场。弗若斯特沙利文咨询公司(Frost & Sullivan)大中华区总裁王文伟(Neil Wang)表示，这两家公司正在与爱立信和诺基亚在本土展开竞争。然而，即便是在这些市场，由于缺乏业内的密切合作伙伴，中国企业集团也有被拒之门外的风险。

4) 华为正在与5G联盟密切合作，其中包括美国电话电报公司(AT&T)和威瑞森(Verizon)等美国公司。但研究咨询机构全球数据(GlobalData)的罗杰斯(Rogers)表示，与日本、韩国和美国之间的大规模合作相比，这些合作就显得微不足道了，因为这些市场的目标是率先推出商业5G服务。

5) 由于获得授权频谱对电信运营商来说十分重要，李认为可能会达成某种妥协，即全球还是采用中低频，而在人口密集的城市中心以超高频作为一种补充手段。

Part 4 Sentence Structure

5. Directions: Combine the following sentences in each group into a complex sentence.

1) What emerges is a picture of an environment where the emphasis is on managing the technology as it spies on people doing their jobs rather than promoting quality service to customers and providing a fair workplace.

2) The American economic system is, organized around a basically private-enterprise, market-oriented economy in which consumers largely determine what shall be produced by spending their money in the marketplace for those goods and services that they want most.

3) Today it is not unusual for a student, even if he works part time at college and full time during the summer, to have $5,000 in loans after four years—loans that he must start to repay within one year after graduation.

4) Advertisement serves directly to assist a rapid distribution of goods at reasonable price, thereby establishing a firm home market and so making it possible to

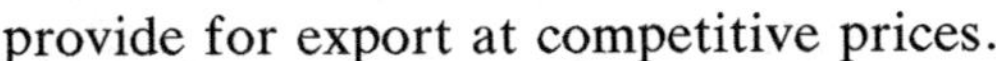

provide for export at competitive prices.

5) Drug dependence is marked first by an increased tolerance, with more of the substance required to produce the desired effect.

Part 5 Academic Writing Skills

6. Directions: Rewrite the following sentences with noun phrases, adjective phrases, or prepositional phrases.

1) Li et al. [24] presented multiple impossible differential attacks on FOX *with better result than* any of the cryptanalysis of FOX known so far.
2) CheckMate, *a program analysis framework for Java*, uses Jchord to instrument lock acquires and releases.
3) Furthermore, *as opposed to* previous works, our technique does not need further information, such as friend relationships or group belongings.
4) The *emergence* of English as the international language of scientific communication has been widely documented.
5) *As shown in Figure 3*, each visible character is actually four characters, superimposed, three of them *visible* only if an associated link is visited.

Unit Three

Satellite Navigation Systems

Section A The Global Positioning System for Military Users: Current Modernization Plans and Alternatives

文章主旨

This article mainly describes the different modernization plans and schedules for the Global Positioning System (GPS). The Department of Defense's (DoD's) GPS satellites will reach the end of their service lives. In order to counter deliberate interference from enemy forces, DoD plans to upgrade its constellation of GPS satellites by generating stronger signals. This text firstly overviews DoD's developing plans in different phases. As a contrast, it also introduces the options of improving military receivers suggested by the Congressional Budget Office (CBO). And then an evaluation to the options has been made. The contrast analysis shows that the military receiver improvements in all the options will be less expensive and yield benefits almost a decade earlier than DoD's plan except that the existing receivers' weight and bulk will be added and stronger M-code signals within the spot-beam and high positioning accuracy offered by the Ⅲ C satellites will be canceled.

教学目标

- To have a thorough understanding of the text.
- To learn how to express ideas with complicated sentences.
- To be able to use the knowledge learned to discuss issues about GPS.
- To drill students in acquiring the central meanings of paragraphs.

学习时间

4 hours (2 hours for the text; 2 hours for discussion)

A. 课堂讲授模块

预习要求

- To learn and recite the new words.
- To grasp the main idea of the text after reading.
- To search for materials related to Bitcoin.

学习时间

2 hours

教学方法

heuristic teaching; project-based teaching; task-driven teaching; group discussion; self-study and peer learning

组织形式

- Let the students work in groups to discuss the text structure and its main idea based on fast reading, and to draw a simple mind-map as well.
- Summarize key technical terms, words and phrases, and sentence patterns in articles involving such technologies as the constellation of GPS, Beidou, inertial navigation systems (INS), iGPS, etc.
- Let the students discuss in groups the learning gains based on their fields of research, and a presentation is expected.
- Analyze the complex sentences and technical issues. Spare some time to respond to any questions from the students.

背景知识

1. What is GPS?

GPS stands for the Global Positioning System. It refers to a system of satellites and receivers that allow people and devices to pinpoint their precise location on the Earth. The heart of the system relies on 24 satellites that orbit the planet twice per day. Devices that are equipped with GPS equipment receive transmissions from at least a few of the satellites and are able to discern very precise positioning data.

The first GPS satellite was launched in 1974 and the 24th was launched in 1994. The system is operated by the United States Department of Defense and its use is free for anyone. New satellites are periodically launched to replace aging ones. As the technology has improved, the cost of devices that include this technology has plummeted while the accuracy has increased. Small portable GPS receivers have become very affordable, and the accuracy is amazing. Accuracy varies based on various factors, but it can be as good as a few yards (meters). Land-based supplemental devices can be used to improve accuracy if higher precision is required.

The application of the GPS is very broad, and as the prices come down the number of uses is increasing. Portable devices are used by fisherman and hikers to help them navigate in the wild. Many new cars are being equipped with GPS systems to help drivers with navigation. The military uses it to guide cruise missiles to pre-specified targets. It's even used for tracking and hunting hobbies, like geocaching.

2. How does GPS work?

GPS satellites circle the earth twice a day in a very precise orbit and transmit signal information to earth. GPS receivers take this information and use triangulation to calculate the user's exact location. Essentially, the GPS receiver compares the time a signal was transmitted by a satellite with the time it was received. The time difference tells the GPS receiver how far away the satellite is. Now, with distance measurements from a few more satellites, the receiver can determine the user's position and display it on the unit's electronic map. A GPS receiver must be locked on to the signal of at least three satellites to calculate a 2D position (latitude and longitude) and track movement. With four or more satellites in view, the receiver can determine the user's 3D position (latitude, longitude and altitude). Once the user's position has been determined, the GPS unit can calculate other information, such as speed, bearing, track, trip distance, distance to destination, sunrise and sunset time and more.

3. The GPS satellite system

The 24 satellites that make up the GPS space segment are orbiting the earth about 12,000 miles above us. They are constantly moving, making two complete orbits in less than 24 hours. These satellites are travelling at speeds of roughly 7,000 miles an hour.

GPS satellites are powered by solar energy. They have backup batteries onboard to keep them running in the event of a solar eclipse, when there's no solar power. Small rocket boosters on each satellite keep them flying in the correct path.

Here are some other interesting facts about the GPS satellites (also called NAVSTAR, the official U.S. Department of Defense name for GPS):

- The first GPS satellite was launched in 1978.
- A full constellation of 24 satellites was achieved in 1994.
- Each satellite is built to last about 10 years. Replacements are constantly being built and launched into orbit.
- A GPS satellite weighs approximately 2,000 pounds and is about 17 feet across with the solar panels extended.
- Transmitter power is only 50 watts or less.

4. The application of GPS

GPS has a variety of applications on land, at sea and in the air. Basically, GPS is usable everywhere except where it's impossible to receive the signal such as inside most buildings, in caves and other subterranean locations, and underwater. The most common airborne applications are for navigation by general aviation and commercial aircraft. At sea, GPS is also typically used for navigation by recreational boaters, commercial fishermen, and professional mariners. Land-based applications are more diverse. The scientific community uses GPS for its precision timing capability and position information.

Surveyors use GPS for an increasing portion of their work. GPS offers cost savings by drastically reducing setup time at the survey site and providing incredible accuracy. Basic survey units, costing thousands of dollars, can offer accuracies down to one meter. More expensive systems are available that can provide accuracies to within a centimeter.

Recreational uses of GPS are almost as varied as the number of recreational sports available. GPS is popular among hikers, hunters, snowmobilers, mountain bikers, and cross-country skiers, just to name a few. Anyone who needs to keep track of where he or she is, to find his or her way to a specified location, or to know what direction and how fast he or she is going can utilize the benefits of the global positioning system.

GPS is now commonplace in automobiles as well. Some basic systems are in place and provide emergency roadside assistance at the push of a button (by transmitting your current position to a dispatch center). More sophisticated systems that show your position on a street map are also available. Currently these systems allow a driver to keep track of where he or she is and suggest the best route to follow to reach a designated location.

5. Other Satellite Navigation Systems

Other satellite navigation systems in use or various states of development include:

GLONASS—Russia's global navigation system. Fully operational worldwide.

Galileo—a global system being developed by the European Union and other partner countries, planned to be operational by 2014 (and fully deployed by 2019).

Beidou/COMPASS—the People's Republic of China's regional system, currently limited to Asia and the West Pacific.

IRNSS—India's regional navigation system, planned to be operational by 2014, covering India and Northern Indian Ocean.

QZSS—Japanese regional system covering Asia and Oceania.

6. BeiDou Navigation Satellite System

The BeiDou Navigation Satellite System (BDS) has been independently constructed and operated by China with an eye to the needs of the country's national security and economic and social development. As a space infrastructure of national significance, BDS provides all-time, all-weather and high-accuracy positioning, navigation and timing services to global users.

Along with the development of the BDS service capability, related products have been widely applied in communication, marine fishery, hydrological monitoring, weather forecasting, surveying, mapping and geographic information, forest fire prevention, time synchronization for communication systems, power dispatching, disaster mitigation and relief, emergency search and rescue, and other fields. These products have been gradually penetrating every aspect of social production and people's life, injecting new vitality into the global economy and social development.

Navigation satellite systems are public resources shared by the whole globe, while the multi-system compatibility and interoperability have become a trend. China has been applying the principle that "BDS is developed by China, and dedicated to the world", serving the development of the Silk Road Economic Belt, and actively pushing forward international cooperation related to BDS. As BDS joins hands with other navigation satellite systems, China works with all other countries, regions and international organizations to promote global satellite navigation development and make BDS further serve the world and benefit mankind.

The BDS development is aimed to build a world-class navigation satellite system to meet the needs of the country's national security as well as economic and social development; to provide continuous, stable and reliable services for global users; to develop the BDS-related industries to support China's economic and social development, as well as improvement of people's living standards; and to enhance international cooperation to share the fruits of the development in the field of satellite navigation, increasing the comprehensive application benefits of Global Navigation Satellite System (GNSS).

In the late 20th century, China started to explore a path to develop a navigation satellite system suitable for its national conditions, and gradually formulated a three-step development strategy: to complete the construction of BDS-1 and provide services to the whole country by the end of 2000, to complete the construction of BDS-2 and provide services to the Asia-Pacific region by the end of 2012; and to complete the construction of the BDS and provide services worldwide around 2020.

Currently, the basic BDS navigation service performance standards are as follows:

- System service coverage: global;
- Positioning accuracy: 10 meters horizontally, 10 meters vertically (95%);
- Velocity measurement accuracy: 0.2 m/s (95%);
- Timing accuracy: 20 nanoseconds (95%);
- System service availability: better than 95%.
- In the Asia-Pacific region, the positioning accuracies are 5 meters horizontally and 5 meters vertically (95%).

The Development Plan: To complete the constellation deployment with the launch

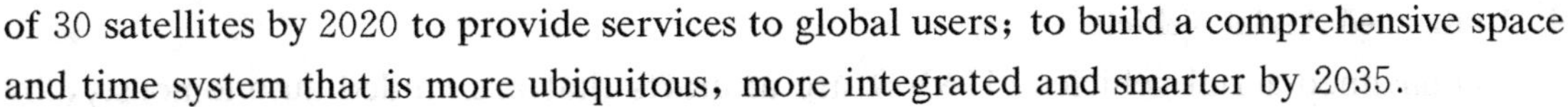

of 30 satellites by 2020 to provide services to global users; to build a comprehensive space and time system that is more ubiquitous, more integrated and smarter by 2035.

7. Congressional Budget Office (CBO)

Since 1975, CBO has produced independent analyses of budgetary and economic issues to support the Congressional budget process. Each year, the agency's economists and budget analysts produce dozens of reports and hundreds of cost estimates for proposed legislation.

CBO is strictly nonpartisan, conducts objective, impartial analysis, and hires its employees solely on the basis of professional competence without regard to political affiliation. CBO does not make policy recommendations, and each report and cost estimate summarizes the methodology underlying the analysis.

CBO's work follows processes specified in the Congressional Budget and Impoundment Control Act of 1974 (which established the agency) or developed by the agency in concert with the House and Senate Budget Committees and the Congressional leadership.

8. Iridium Satellite System

The Iridium satellite network includes three principal components which include the satellite network, the ground stations and the satellite phones and data units. Voice and data messages can be routed anywhere in the world by the Iridium network. Calls are relayed from the satellite phone or data unit on the ground to one of the Iridium satellites. It is then relayed from one satellite to another then down to an appropriate ground station. The call is then transferred to the public voice network or Internet when it reaches the recipient.

The Iridium satellite constellation is a large group of satellites providing voice and data coverage to satellite phones, pagers and integrated transceivers over Earth's entire surface. Iridium Communications Inc. owns and operates the constellation and sells equipment and access to its services. It was originally conceived by Bary Bertiger, Dr. Ray Leopold and Ken Peterson in late 1987 (and protected by patents by Motorola in their names in 1988) and then developed by Motorola on a fixed-price contract from July 29, 1993 to November 1, 1998 when the system became operational and commercially available.

The constellation consists of 66 active satellites in orbit, and additional spare satellites to serve in case of failure. Satellites are in low Earth orbit at a height of approximately 485 mi (781 km) and inclination of 86.4°. Orbital velocity of the satellites is 17,000 mph (27,000 km/h). Satellites communicate with neighboring satellites via K band inter-satellite links. Each satellite can have four inter-satellite links: two to neighbors fore and aft in the same orbital plane, and two to satellites in neighboring planes to either side.

9. Unmanned Aerial Vehicle

Unmanned aerial vehicles (UAVs) are aircrafts that are guided autonomously, by remote control, or by both means and that carry sensors, target designators, offensive ordnance, or electronic transmitters designed to interfere with or destroy enemy targets. Unencumbered by crew, life-support systems, and the design-safety requirements of manned aircraft, UAVs can be remarkably efficient, offering substantially greater range and endurance than equivalent manned systems.

UAVs are descended from target drones and remotely piloted vehicles (RPVs) employed by the military forces of many countries in the decades immediately after World War II. Modern UAVs debuted as an important weapons system in the early 1980s, when the Israeli Defense Forces fitted small drones resembling large model airplanes with trainable television and infrared cameras and with target designators for laser-guided munitions, all downlinked to a control station. Rendered undetectable by their small size and quiet engines, these vehicles proved effective in battlefield surveillance and target designation. Other armed forces learned from the Israeli success, notably the United States, which purchased some of the early Israeli models or produced them under license. The most important American tactical UAV—and one that is representative of trends in the development of these aircraft—is the MQ-1 Predator, which first flew in 1994 and entered service the following year. The Predator, with a length of 26 feet 8 inches (8 metres) and a wingspan of 41 feet 8 inches (12.5 metres), is powered by a piston engine driving a pusher propeller. It flies at 80 miles (130 km) per hour and has an endurance of 24 hours. In addition to visible and infrared television, it carries synthetic aperture radar and passive electronic sensors, and it can also carry antitank missiles. Control inputs and sensor outputs are transmitted via communications satellite. A larger, turboprop-powered derivative of the Predator, the MQ-9 Reaper, has improved performance and carries a larger ordnance load. Both the Predator and the Reaper have been used in the conflicts in Iraq and Afghanistan and have been purchased by allies of the United States.

重点词汇

1. **constellation** /ˌkɒnstɪˈleɪʃən/ *n*. a group of stars that forms a shape in the sky and has a name 星座
   - ➢ Analysis by the Congressional Budget Office (CBO) indicates that an alternative approach—namely, improving military receivers to retain the GPS signal even in the presence of such jamming—would be less expensive than DoD's plan for upgrading its ***constellation*** of GPS satellites. (Para.1)
   - ➢ A ***constellation*** of qualities made her particularly suited to the job.
2. **thereby** /ˌðeəˈbaɪ/ *adv*. used to introduce the result of the action or situation

mentioned 因此，由此[正式]

➢ ... and ***thereby*** less useful to personnel operating on foot. (Para. 1)

➢ He became a citizen, ***thereby*** gaining the right to vote.

3. **incorporate** /ɪnˈkɔːpəreɪt/ *v*. ... something (in/into/within something) to include something so that it forms a part of something 使并入[正式](SYN) integrate/infuse (... into ...)

➢ ... they could ***incorporate*** the substantial gains that have been achieved ***in*** miniaturization in other applications. (Para. 1)

➢ There's more than one way to learn, so be sure to ***incorporate*** different methods ***in*** your training.

4. **miniaturization** /ˌmɪnətʃəraɪˈzeɪʃn/ *n*. (also miniaturisation) the act of making a much smaller version of something 小型化，微型化

➢ ... they could incorporate the substantial gains that have been achieved in ***miniaturization*** in other applications. (Para. 1)

➢ Electronic dictionaries are the by-product of the inexorable progress of computerization, ***miniaturization*** and nanotechnology which has meant that one of their biggest advantages is their small size.

5. **transmit** /trænzˈmɪt/ *v*. transmit (something) (from ...) (to ...) to send an electronic signal, radio or television broadcast, etc. 传导(声音、电子信号等)(SYN) transfer, relay, transport, channel, convey, etc.

➢ The GPS uses a constellation of at least 24 satellites, each of which ***transmits*** precise data on the time and its location. (Para. 2)

➢ In a UHF passive RFID system, a reader ***transmits*** an unmodulated continuous wave (CW) to tags, which not only provides energy to tags but also serves as the carrier of tag backscatter signals.

6. **swamp** /swɒmp/ *v*. fill with water 淹没(SYN) overwhelm (Para. 3), flood, fill (up)...

➢ However, because the GPS signal from space is very weak by the time it reaches Earth (like the light from a 25-watt lightbulb shining 12,500 miles away), the system can easily be ***swamped*** by interference. (Para. 2)

➢ Their electronic navigation failed and a huge wave ***swamped*** the boat.

7. **initiate** /ɪˈnɪʃieɪt/ *v*. (formal) to make something begin 使开始，发起

➢ In 2000, DoD ***initiated*** plans to reduce the system's susceptibility to intentional interference. (Para. 3)

➢ Last spring, the United States ***initiated*** economic and diplomatic sanctions.

8. **susceptibility** /səˌseptəˈbɪləti/ *n*. the state of being very likely to be influenced, harmed or affected by something 易受影响(或损害)的状况，敏感性，过敏性

➢ In 2000, DoD initiated plans to reduce the system's ***susceptibility*** to intentional interference. (Para. 3)

- ***Susceptibility*** to acid depends in part on the type of calcium carbonate the animal makes, the researchers found.

9. illuminate /ɪˈluːmɪneɪt/ *v.* to shine light on something 照亮[正式]

- Those satellites will transmit signals with the same strength as Ⅲ B satellites and will be able to use the spotbeam to ***illuminate*** an area with a diameter of 600 miles on the Earth's surface with signals 100 times stronger than those of current GPS satellites. (Para. 5)
- The light shines on from over there and ***illuminates*** the stage.

10. field /fiːld/ *v.* to put into the field, such as field an army, field a team, etc. 派遣,组建,装配

- ... no users have been able to benefit from them because DoD does not have the ability to monitor or control the signals, nor has it ***fielded*** receivers to process the signals. (Para. 6)
- Moreover, to make the planned system useful, M-code-capable receivers will need to be ***fielded*** as well. (Para. 6)

11. yield /jiːld/ *v.* to produce or provide something, for example a profit, result or crop 出产(作物),产生(收益、效益等),提供(SYN) produce, acquire, gain, get

- All three options would cost less to carry out than DoD's plan and would ***yield*** military receivers with greater antijamming capability earlier. (Para. 16)
- Really focused pronunciation practice can ***yield*** great results.

12. augment /ɔːgˈment/ *v.* to increase the amount, value, size, etc. of something 增加[正式](SYN) improve, increase, grow

- Option 1 would ***augment*** military receivers to provide users with a better ability to keep track of their location in jamming environments. (Para. 17)
- While searching for a way to ***augment*** the family income, she began making dolls.

13. entail /ɪnˈteɪl/ *v.* to involve something that cannot be avoided 牵连,导致[正式]

→同样前缀的词还有: enable (Para. 21), ensure (Para. 24)

- But, designing and integrating such miniaturized devices for and into existing receivers would take time and could ***entail*** costs not included in CBO's estimates. (Para. 25)
- Such a decision would ***entail*** a huge political risk in the midst of the presidential campaign.

14. forgo /fɔːˈgəʊ/ (also forego) *v.* to decide not to have or do something that you would like to have or do 放弃[正式](SYN) abandon

- ***Forgoing*** the Ⅲ C satellites would also mean the loss of the ability to determine position to within about 6 inches for civilian users under all of the options and for military users under Option 1. (Para. 26)

➢ You may have to ***forego*** a vacation or work 12-hour days to complete an important project.

重点短语

1. in the presence of: with someone present and watching or supervising 在……面前,有某人在场

➢ ... namely, improving military receivers to retain the GPS signal even ***in the presence of*** such jamming. (Para. 1)

➢ The meeting will take place ***in the presence of*** the Minister of Education and Culture.

➢ Courage is finding the strength to move ahead ***in the presence of*** fear.

2. as of: from, at, or until a given time 自从,截止到

This idiom was first used in business but came into more general use.

➢ Ten satellites capable of transmitting M-code signals were already in orbit ***as of*** August 2011. (Para. 3)

➢ ***As of*** now, I'm not sure how I'll vote.

➢ ***As of*** Sunday August 28, 2011, Hurricane Irene was downgraded to Tropical Storm Irene.

3. capable of: having the ability to do something 能够

➢ The department has already purchased—but not yet launched—10 of those GPS satellites ***capable of*** transmitting M-code signals. (Para. 4)

➢ In the wake of developments in science and technology, man has become more ***capable of*** conquering nature.

➢ Show your teacher what you are ***capable of***.

4. equip sth. with sth.: to add a piece of equipment to something 装备,配备有……

➢ For the final phase, the department's plan calls for an initial purchase of 8 GPS Ⅲ C satellites, which will ***be equipped with*** a special antenna capable of focusing the M-code signals in a "spotbeam". (Para. 5)

➢ In the modern international business activities, employees have to ***equip with*** the knowledge structure and ability.

➢ How do we ***equip*** people ***with*** the skills those jobs require?

5. confine sth. to sth.: to restrict something to a particular person or thing; to limit the scope of something 限定于,局限于

➢ First, under each option, DoD would purchase 40 GPS Ⅲ satellites (the same number as in DoD's plan) but ***confine*** those purchases ***to*** the Ⅲ A model. (Para. 15)

➢ Judges may be trained to ***confine*** themselves ***to*** the legally relevant facts before them.

➢ Quantum dots are man-made atoms that ***confine*** electrons ***to*** a small space.

6. **take advantage of**：to utilize or avail oneself of something to the fullest possible extent 利用(SYN) capitalize on

➢ By CBO's estimates，the total cost for those three common items is \$17.9 billion from 2012 through 2025—which is the amount to maintain，modernize，and control the GPS constellation through 2030 and to field military receivers that can ***take*** full ***advantage of*** the M-code signal.（Para.15）

➢ Try to ***take advantage of*** every opportunity that comes your way.

➢ Let's ***take advantage of*** the good weather and go hiking.

7. **result from**：to exist，emerge，or occur as a direct consequence or outcome of something 起因于

➢ The extent of the improvements in military receivers' capability ***resulting from*** this option would be somewhat greater than that from Option 1 and could be realized just as quickly—by 2018.（Para.20）

➢ It will be interesting to see what ***results from*** your efforts.

➢ Knowledge is gained from assiduity，unwisdom is ***resulted from*** sluttery!

8. **comprised of**：made up of（something）；consisting of（something）由……组成

➢ The earliest benefits would probably come once the constellation of 18 GPS Ⅲ satellites—***comprised of*** 8 Ⅲ A and 10 Ⅲ B satellites—is in orbit，scheduled for 2022，but only small numbers of military receivers capable of processing the stronger M-code signals would be in the field then.（Para.22）

➢ Your grade is ***comprised of*** several factors，such as homework，projects，and test scores.

➢ The committee was ***comprised of*** representatives from all areas.

9. **line of sight**：an imaginary line that stretches between your eye and the object that you are looking at(游戏或射击中的)视线

➢ That fuller coverage would virtually ensure that receivers had a ***line of sight*** to at least one satellite，even in mountainous terrain and urban settings where tall buildings block the view of the sky.（Para.24）

➢ He was trying to keep out of the bird's ***line of sight***.

➢ These calculations might be based on visibility（whether the tag is in the sensor's ***line of sight***），the signal strength，or the amount of time it takes the signal to travel from the tag to the sensor.

难句解析

1. As a first step towards providing some protection against jamming，DoD decided that GPS satellites would transmit additional signals，available only to military

users, each of which covered a wider range of frequencies than those already being transmitted. (Para.3)

Paraphrase: DoD's first step for anti-jamming was its decision that only military users would have the access to GPS satellites emitting additional signals. Compared with signals already being transmitted, these added ones have a wider range of frequencies.

解析： that 引导的宾语从句中，又有 which 引导的非限制性定语从句，available only to military users 为插入语，可以理解为 which are available only to military users，也是 additional signals 的修饰限定成分，说明这些信号只能供军方使用，且每个信号的带宽频率都更强。而句子开头的 as 短语，进一步阐释了这种操作的真正目的是提供干扰防护措施，而这仅是第一步而已。

翻译： 作为反干扰保护措施的第一步，DoD 决定增加 GPS 卫星的传输信号，并只将增加的信号提供给军方用户，与之前使用的信号相比，该信号覆盖的带宽更广。

2. Although 10 satellites capable of transmitting the harder-to-jam M-code signals are currently in orbit (the first one since 2005), no users have been able to benefit from them because DoD does not have the ability to monitor or control the signals, nor has it field receivers to process the signals. (Para.6)

Paraphrase: Even if 10 satellites are now functional, users cannot gain any benefit from them, because DoD cannot check or control the signals, and does not have receivers equipped to analyze them. These 10 satellites (the first one in orbit since 2005) can send M-code signals that are harder to be jammed.

解析： although 引导让步状语从句，主句中又嵌套有 because 引导的原因状语从句，且有 nor 开头的部分倒装句。让步状语从句中，capable of doing something 修饰 satellites，意指这是优势，但可惜没有很好地加以利用，no users 用否定词开头，强调无一例外，主句用了现在完成时，表示从 2005 年至今，这么长的时间，花费了巨资，却毫无用处！后面的原因状语从句给出了两个造成这种现状的理由：首先是美国国防部没有监测或控制这些信号的能力；其次是接收机也没有装备到位，无法进行信号分析。

翻译： 虽然目前在轨卫星中能够发射 M 码信号的卫星(自 2005 年首颗发射)已经达到 10 颗，但是因为 DoD 没有监测或控制该信号的能力，也没有配备处理该信号的接收机，因此还没有用户能够从中受益。

3. If the satellites and receivers performed as planned, the combination of all of the upgrades proposed by DoD would enable military receivers to operate in the presence of much stronger jamming signals than they can withstand today. (Para.7)

Paraphrase: If the satellites and receivers can work according to the plan, DoD's all upgrades propositions would be able to let the military receivers work under much stronger jamming signals than the current.

解析： if 引导虚拟条件句，从句是过去式，主句为 would＋do。主句中主语之后的 proposed by DoD 为过去分词短语作定语，相当于 which was proposed by DoD。主句后面有 than 引导的比较状语从句。

翻译：如果卫星和接收机按计划运行，那么 DoD 提出的所有升级建议就能使军用接收机在比现在更强的干扰信号下工作。

4. By CBO's estimates, the total cost for those three common items is $17.9 billion from 2012 through 2025—which is the amount to maintain, modernize, and control the GPS constellation through 2030 and to field military receivers that can take full advantage of the M-code signal. (Para. 15)

Paraphrase: According to CBO's calculation, the total cost for the mentioned three options is $17.9 billion from 2012 to 2025, including the expense of the maintenance, modernization and management of the GPS constellation before 2030 and of the equipment of the M-code signal-processing military receivers.

解析：破折号的用法，进一步解释说明。which 引导的定语从句，还是主系表结构。to maintain, modernize, and control ... and to field ... 中的 to do 动词不定式表示目的，说明这笔钱的用途有两个：GPS 星群的维护和军事接收机的装备到位；此外，to maintain, modernize, and control ... 与 to field military receivers ... 是并列结构。that 引导限制性定语从句，修饰 receivers。take full advantage of 固定短语，指充分利用……

翻译：据 CBO 估计，2012 到 2025 年间完成上述三项所需的费用总额为 179 亿美元，这包括到 2030 年前对 GPS 星座进行的维护、现代化改造、运管等费用，以及部署能够处理 M 码信号的军用接收机的费用。

5. The improvement would come from new antennas—capable of rejecting signals from jammers—and from the integration of very small inertial navigation systems, which would reduce location errors introduced by interference and enable users on the move to determine their position accurately even after losing the GPS signal entirely. (Para. 17)

Paraphrase: New antennas and the integration of very small inertial navigation systems are the two improvements. The former would be able to disrupt signals from jammers; the latter would reduce location errors which are caused by interference, and make users on the move to locate their position precisely even after losing the GPS signal entirely.

解析：破折号的用法，两个破折号相当于两个小括号，或者两个逗号，是句子的插入语，可以补充成 which is capable of。改进和完善有两个方面，一个是新天线，另一个是惯性导航系统的使用。which 引导非限定性定语从句，修饰 small inertial navigation systems。从句中有 and 引导的并列成分，introduced by interference 为过去分词短语作后置定语，修饰 location errors。enable somebody to do something 是固定搭配，意为"使某人做某事"。这个定语从句阐释了惯性导航系统的两个优点。determine one's position 在文中出现较多次，意为"测定某人(某物)的方位"。

翻译：这种改进是通过采用新式天线，并整合一些小型的惯性导航系统来实现的。前者具有抗干扰信号的能力；后者则可以帮助运动中的用户在完全丧失 GPS 信号的一定时间内仍能准确测定其方位，且可以减少干扰造成的定位误差。

写作技巧

Comparison and Contrast

Overview

In writing, comparison discusses elements that are similar, while contrast that are different. Thus, a compare-and-contrast essay analyzes two subjects by comparing or contrasting them, or both.

To choose two or more subjects connected in a meaningful way is the key to a good compare-and-contrast essay. We conduct the comparison or contrast to illuminate unexpected similarities or subtle differences rather than state the obvious. For instance, you would not pick apples and oranges if you wanted to contrast two subjects; instead, two types of oranges or two types of apples may be your best choice to highlight subtle differences. You will see Red Delicious apples are sweet, while Granny Smiths are tart and acidic. Drawing differentiation between elements in a similar category will increase the audience's understanding of that category. Likewise, to focus on comparison, we would choose to compare how apples or oranges are similar though they seem at first not to be related.

The compare-and-contrast essay starts with a thesis that clearly states the two subjects to be compared, contrasted, or both and the reason for doing so. Comparing, contrasting, or both may be the focus. The point of comparing and contrasting is to provide useful knowledge to the reader, no matter what. The essay can be developed in a block-to-block or point-to-point way. The former discusses one and then the other according to subjects themselves while the latter each subject in relation to each point according to individual points.

It is helpful to have some phrases that will cue the reader to such analysis. See the following table of words and phrases of comparison and contrast.

Comparison	Contrast
one similarity	one difference
another similarity	another difference
both	conversely
like	in contrast
likewise	unlike

(Continued)

Comparison	Contrast
similarly	while
in a similar fashion	whereas

To illustrate this, we will take two paragraphs for an example.

Sample Section Analysis

➢ **Sample Paragraphs**

(S1)Compared with DoD's plan, the options would yield greater improvements in reception and would yield improvements sooner. (S2)Under DoD's plan, the full benefit of the increased M-code signal power of the Ⅲ C satellites would not be fully realized until 2030, when the 16th Ⅲ C satellite could be in orbit. (S3) The earliest benefits would probably come once the constellation of 18 GPS Ⅲ satellites—comprised of 8 Ⅲ A and 10 Ⅲ B satellites—is in orbit, scheduled for 2022, but only small numbers of military receivers capable of processing the stronger M-code signals would be in the field then. (S4) While the Ⅲ C satellites were being placed in orbit, the benefit of their stronger signals would be unavailable to users until sufficient numbers of M-code-capable receivers were fielded, possibly no earlier than 2026.

(S5) In contrast, the technologies included in CBO's options—those for improved antennas for GPS receivers, small inertial navigation devices, and iGPS—have already been developed. (S6)The fielding of ancillary devices to augment existing military GPS receivers could begin in a few years, with appreciable numbers of improved receivers in the field by 2018. (S7) Consequently, the options could increase the military's antijamming capability eight years before large numbers of M-code receivers could be in the hands of military users under DoD's plan.

➢ **Analysis**

These two paragraphs make a contrast between DoD's plan and the options from two angles, namely, improvements and schedule. It is developed in a block-to-block way. The first sentence serves as the topic sentence of both paragraphs, followed by a detailed analysis of DoD's plan in Paragraph 1 and that of CBO's options in Paragraph 2.

In terms of improvements, DoD's plan is mainly around M-code signal power and receivers. The author deconstructs the plan from three aspects which are "the full benefit" (S2), "the earliest benefits" (S3) and "the benefit of stronger signals" (S4). By contrast, CBO's technologies are more advanced as illustrated by "improved antennas" (S5), "small inertial navigation devices" (S5), "iGPS" (S5), and ancillary devices (S6). The author concludes with the overall effect of CBO's options which is the increased antijamming capabilities (S7).

Distinction in devices are not only shown in quality but also in quantity. Phrases like "only a small number of military receivers" (S3) are outcompeted by those like "appreciable numbers of improved receivers".

Regarding the schedule, the author employs specific and exact wording to show sharp differences. In paragraph 1, words like "2030""2022" and "no earlier than 2026" indicate that this plan is a dead weight. CBO's plan, on the other hand, runs in the foreseeable future. Words like "have already been developed" (S5), "in a few years" (S6), "by 2018" (S6), and "eight years before" (S7) are such a case in point.

Get started on your own

Directions: Read Paras. 17 – 21 carefully and write an analysis paragraph by identifying "Comparison and Contrast".

篇章分析

This article starts with an overview of the whole passage under "Highlights". For DoD's plan, the current modernization plan, its background information, purpose, implement phases and software development plan are presented to provide readers enough knowledge about its ins and outs. Then the author works on its evaluation, pointing out its planned performance and benefits for military and civilian users. However, costly expense, negligence in receiver improvements and lack of coordination are great concerns. That is why CBO's options are proposed afterwards. This alternative includes three options, each boasting its competitive edge. Meanwhile, they have a lot in common in terms of systems and cost. To give readers a clear picture, each option is elaborated with more detailed information. In the last few paragraphs, the author examines the options carefully. Advantages of these new plans lie in more advanced devices and performances and earlier implementation. Disadvantages are evident in terms of purchasing hardware additions, discarding improvements offered by the Ⅲ C satellites and depending on commercial satellite constellation and support network.

We visualize the text structure by means of a mind map.

The Global Positioning System for Military Users:
Current Modernization Plans and Alternatives

- **Overview (Para. 1)**
- **DoD's plan (Paras. 2 – 10)**
  - Background information (Para. 2)
  - Purpose(Para. 3)
  - Purchase plan (Paras. 4 – 5)

- ○ Software development (Para. 6)
- ○ Advantages (Paras. 7 - 8)
- ○ Disadvantages (Paras. 9 - 10)
- ● **CBO's options (Paras. 11 - 21)**
  - ○ Introduction (Para. 11)
  - ○ General introduction to each option (Paras. 12 - 14)
  - ○ Commonalities among options (Paras. 15 - 16)
  - ○ Detailed description of each option (Paras. 17 - 21)
- ● **Comparison of the plans (Paras. 22 - 27)**
  - ○ Advantages (Paras. 22 - 24)
  - ○ Disadvantages (Paras. 25 - 27)

课堂提问

- ➢ According to the text, what plans would be included in the GPS modernization improvement raised by DoD?
- ➢ According to the description of the text, why did DoD decide that GPS satellites would transmit M-code signals?
- ➢ How many phases are there in DoD's Plan of developing and purchasing the new satellites? What are they?
- ➢ Why did CBO provide three options?
- ➢ What are the options developed by CBO?

教学建议

- ➢ According to the text, some modernization plans and other options are proposed as for the GPS enhancement. Students are supposed to fill a table related to them, so that they would know more about the advantages and disadvantages of different options.
- ➢ Students are advised to conduct an extensive reading of the latter part to gain a better understanding of how GPS receivers work.

B. 课堂讨论模块

学习时间

2 hours

讨论内容

- ➢ To ask students to present the steps of COMPASS deployment.

- To exemplify the application of Chinese satellite navigation system in our lives.

教学方法

heuristic teaching; group discussion; class presentation

组织形式

- To divide students into several groups and choose a student from each group to show his or her PPT on the applications of satellite navigation system in our lives.
- To allow students to ask any question concerning the content of the text.

参考问题

- What is GPS?
- What can GPS be used for? Can you show one or two examples to illustrate the applications of GPS in our lives?
- Besides GPS, what other navigation systems do you know?

课后练习

Refer to the exercises in Unit Three of the textbook.

练习答案

Part 1 Reading Comprehension

1. Directions: Do the following statements agree with the information given in the reading passage? In blanks 1)- 5), choose

TRUE	if the statement agrees with the information.
FALSE	if the statement contradicts the information.
NOT GIVEN	if there is no such information in the statement.

1) T (Para.3) 2) F (Para.9) 3) NG (Para.15) 4) T (Para.22) 5) F (Para.26)

2. Directions: Paraphrase the following sentences.

1) It is the DoD's decision that only military users would have the access to GPS satellites emitting additional signals. Compared with signals already being transmitted, these additional ones have a wider range of frequencies.

2) Signals transmitted from current satellites are possible to locate military users and civilian users within 10 feet. However, the signals transmitted by GPS Ⅲ A satellites allow the location precision to be within 3 feet.

3) In the military forces, handheld receivers are usually used by the Army and the Marines. Therefore, CBO concentrated on them.

4) DoD would go on to develop the ground control system to control current M-code-transmitting GPS satellites (IIR-M and IIF) and the newer GPS Ⅲ A satellites.

5) Under the three options, those savings would be balanced by the cost of improving receivers. Thus, net savings for Option 1, Option 2 and Option 3 would be about \$2 billion, \$3 billion and more than \$1 billion respectively.

Part 2 Words and Expressions

3. Directions: Choose proper words from the following word bank, and fill in blanks in their right forms.

1) integrate 2) onerous 3) generates 4) envisioning 5) confined

6) was ... illuminated 7) swamp 8) susceptible 9) incorporate 10) yielded

Part 3 Translation

4. Directions: Translate the following sentences from the reading passage into Chinese.

1) 这些卫星(GPS-Ⅲ C卫星)不但具有与GPS-Ⅲ B卫星相同的信号传输强度,而且还能使用点波束将信号发射到地球上一个直径达600英里的区域,使其信号强度比现在GPS卫星信号强100倍。

2) 据美国国会预算办公室(CBO)估计,从2012年到2025年,完成上述3点所需的费用总额将达到179亿美元,包括2030年以前用于GPS卫星的维护、改造以及控制的费用,以及安装可以完全发挥M码信号优势的接收机的费用。

3) CBO的备选方案不会像DoD的计划那样为民用GPS带来性能提升,同时,这个方案也放弃了GPS-Ⅲ C卫星对所有用户定位精度上的改进。

4) 此外,因为可以经常接收并更新数据,iGPS接收机用户与未来可能用到GPS-Ⅲ C卫星传输数据的用户具有几乎相同的定位精度,但前者却会早实现若干年。

5) 但是,设计和组装这些缩微设备到现有的接收机中尚需时间,而且可能会带来超过CBO估算的额外成本。

Part 4 Sentence Structure

5. Directions: Combine the following sentences in each group into a complex sentence.

1) The worker who gets a promotion, the student whose grades improve, the foreigner who learns a new language—all these are examples of people who have measurable results to show their efforts.

2) The current passion for making children compete against their classmates or against the clock produces a two-layer system, in which competitive A-types seem in some way better than their B type fellows.

3) The debate was launched by the Government, which invited anyone with an opinion of the BBC—including ordinary listeners and viewers to say what was good or bad about the Corporation, and even whether they thought it was worth keeping.

4) His colleague, Michael Beer, says that far too many companies have applied re-engineering in a mechanistic fashion, chopping out costs without giving sufficient thought to long-term profitability.

5) A survey of news stories in 1996 reveals that the antiscience tag has been attached to many other groups as well, from authorities who advocated the elimination of the last remaining stocks of smallpox virus to Republicans who advocated decreased funding for basic research.

Part 5 Academic Writing Skills

6. **Directions:** Find as many synonyms as possible to the following italicized words and phrases in the sentences.

1) An attacker must locate first the target before *transmitting* jamming signal.
2) The optimal beamforming vectors at the eavesdropper are given by SU *to confuse* the eavesdropper.
3) Figure 10 shows that a subgraph, *consisting of* nodes painted in orange or dark green, is disconnected from other categorized nodes.
4) Specifically, the dimensions of the first two radiating structures were set, as in [8], so that the antenna would resonate at frequencies *close to* 2.5 and 3.5 GHz, thereby *yielding* a 2.3 - 3.8 GHz operational band-width, which covers the WiFi 2.4-GHz and the mobile WiMAX 2.3-, 2.5-, 3.3-, and 3.5-GHz frequency bands.
5) The results demonstrate that the proposed narrow-size IFA can operate in all the allocated WiFi and WiMAX frequency bands *while providing near-omnidirectional coverage in the horizontal plane*.

Unit Four
Internet of Things

Section A Panopticon as a Metaphor of the Internet of Things—Why Not? But If It Were the Opposite?

文章主旨

This article attempts to provoke reader's thought on the Internet of Things and the future society. The word "panopticon" was used to describe IoT, which brings benefits, challenges and even risks. But the author is not pessimistic about the future.

教学目标

- To have a clear understanding of what "panopticon" is, and why the author use "panopticon" to describe the society with IoT.
- To grasp the main idea and figure out the structure of the article.
- To master the words and expressions related to IoT.
- To discuss issues about IoT.
- To cultivate writing ability.

学习时间

4 hours (2 hours for the text; 2 hours for discussion)

A. 课堂讲授模块

预习要求

- To learn and recite the new words.
- To grasp the main idea of the text after reading.
- To search for materials related to IoT.

学习时间

2 hours

教学方法

heuristic teaching; project-based teaching; task-driven teaching; group discussion; self-study and peer learning

组织形式

- Let the students work in groups to discuss the text structure and its main idea based on fast reading, and to draw a simple mind-map as well.
- Summarize key technical terms, words and phrases, and sentence patterns in articles involving IoT.
- Let the students discuss in groups the learning gains based on their fields of research, and a presentation is expected.
- Analyze the complex sentences and technical issues. Give feedback to any questions asked by the students.

背景知识

1. Yongmou Liu: *Totalitarianism or Democracy: The Preference of the Internet of Things and its Risk, from the Perspective of Panopticon*

This article is the article mentioned in the first sentence of Para. 1. The abstract of this article is as follows:

Abstract: The Panopticon is the famous metaphor in network research, being characteristic of Jeremy Bentham and Michel Foucault. Compared with Internet, the Internet of Things (IoT) accords better with panopticon in operation target, mechanism and pattern, and so IoT has strong ability of electronic monitoring and surveillance (EM/S). If no restrain in the use of IoT as an instrument of EM/S, it is possible for IoT to become a domineering tool. So, we should precaution political risk of IoT with multifold measures.

2. Rob van Kranenburg

Rob van Kranenburg (1964) is the Founder of Council, the internet of things. eu at IERC IoT Research Cluster of the EU Commission and today he is in the Top 100 IoT Influencers list.

He wrote *The Internet of Things. A critique of ambient technology and the all-seeing network of RFID*, Network Notebooks 02, Institute of Network Cultures. He is co-founder of bricolabs. Together with Christian Nold he published Situated Technologies Pamphlets 8: *The Internet of People for a Post-Oil World*. Rob is co-editor of Enabling Things to Talk Designing IoT solutions with the IoT Architectural Reference Model, Springer Open Access. He works as Ecosystem Manager for the EU projects

Tagitsmart and Next Generation Internet. And he is a DeTao Master IoT.

3. David Brin

David Brin is best known for shining light—plausibly and entertainingly—on technology, society, and countless challenges confronting our rambunctious civilization. His best-selling novels include *The Postman* (filmed in 1997) plus explorations of our near-future in Earth and Existence. Other novels are translated into 25+ languages. His short stories explore vividly speculative ideas.

Brin's nonfiction book *The Transparent Society* won the American Library Association's Freedom of Speech Award for exploring 21st Century concerns about security, secrecy, accountability and privacy.

As a scientist, tech-consultant and world-known author, he speaks, advises, and writes widely on topics from national defense and homeland security to astronomy and space exploration, SETI and nanotechnology, future/prediction, creativity, and philanthropy. Urban Developer Magazine named him one of four World's Best Futurists, and he was appraised as "#1 influencer" in Onalytica's Top 100 report of Artificial Intelligence influencers, brands & publications.

The article concerned in Para. 2 about David Brin is *The Transparent Society: Will Technology Force Us to Choose Between Privacy and Freedom?* (Basic Books, 06/01/1999, ISBN-13: 978-0738201443).

4. Sean Dodson

Sean Dodson is a senior lecturer in journalism at Leeds Metropolitan University. He is also a journalist and writer and has been covering the social uses of technology for over 10 years. He has also worked as an assistant producer at the Guardian and a researcher for the Sunday Times, as well as contributing to a wide range of titles including Wired, Design Week, UK Press Gazette, The South China Morning Post and the Melbourne Age.

5. Jeremy Bentham

Jeremy Bentham (born February 15, 1748, London, England—died June 6, 1832, London), English Philosopher, economist, and theoretical jurist, the founder of modern utilitarianism, an ethical theory holding that actions are morally right if they tend to promote happiness or pleasure (and morally wrong if they tend to promote unhappiness or pain) among all those affected by them.

Jeremy Bentham is important for being one of the founders of modern utilitarianism since the late 18th century, for his defense of psychological and ethical hedonism, and for his far-reaching proposals for the reform of Parliament, the legal code, the judiciary, and the prison system in Britain.

6. Michel Foucault

Michel Foucault, in full Paul-Michel Foucault, (born October 15, 1926, Poitiers,

France—died June 25, 1984, Paris), French historian and philosopher, associated with the structuralist and post-structuralist movements. He has had strong influence not only (or even primarily) in philosophy but also in a wide range of humanistic and social scientific disciplines. He is one of the most influential and controversial scholars of the post-World War Ⅱ period.

7. Jensen and Draffan

Derrick Jensen is the author of *Walking on Water: Reading, Writing and Revolution*; *The Culture of Make Believe*; *A Language Older than Words*; *Listening to the Land: Conversations about Nature, Culture, and Eros*; and co-author of *Railroads & Clearcuts*. *The Culture of Make Believe* was one of two finalists for the 2003 J. Anthony Lukas Book Prize. He writes for The New York Times Magazine, Audubon, and The Sun among many others.

George Draffan is a forest activist, public interest investigator, and corporate muckraker. He is the author of *The Elite Consensus: A Primer on Corporate Power*, and co-author of *Railroads & Clearcuts*. For the past 15 years he has provided research services and training to citizens and public interest groups that are investigating and challenging corporate power. Some of his work can be found at Endgame, a project of the Public Information Network (www.endgame.org)

The article concerned in Para. 7 about Jensen and Draffan is: Derrick Jensen, George Draffan, *Welcome to the Machine: Science, Surveillance, and the Culture of Control*, Thomson Gale, 10/11/2005.

8. Bruce Sterling

Bruce Sterling (1954) is an American science fiction author, journalist, and futurist. He is considered one of the founders of the cyberpunk movement along with William Gibson, John Shirley, and others. He is also included in the cyberpunk anthology *Mirrorshades*. Sterling's first ever science fiction story, *Man-Made Self*, was sold in 1976. He first became famous by hosting annual Christmas event to present digital art.

9. Spime

Spime, coined by Bruce Sterling, means "an object that can be remotely tracked through space and time".

重点词汇

1. **surveillance** /sɜːˈveɪləns/ *n*. the act of carefully watching a person suspected of a crime or a place where a crime may be committed(对犯罪嫌疑人或可能发生犯罪的地方的)监视
   - ➢ The Panopticon is used as a metaphor for describing a "***surveillance*** society" where technology is extensively and routinely used to track and record human

activities and movements in ways which are invisible to ordinary people as they are watched and monitored. (Para. 1)

➢ The police are keeping the suspects under constant ***surveillance***.

➢ Why would you need a ***surveillance*** camera in a brokerage firm?

2. **ubiquitous** /juːˈbɪkwɪtəs/ *adj*. seeming to be everywhere or in several places at the same time; very common 似乎无所不在的，十分普遍的

➢ The City of Control is a place where the deployment of radio frequency identification tags (RFID) have become not just commonplace but ***ubiquitous***. (Para. 3)

➢ Is there no escape from the ***ubiquitous*** cigarette smoke in restaurants?

3. **render** /ˈrendə(r)/ *v*. to cause somebody/something to be in a particular state or condition 使成为，使变得，使处于某状态

➢ Notions of public and private have begun to dissolve; or are ***rendered*** irrelevant; notions of property are rapidly being rethought. (Para. 3)

➢ Hundreds of people were ***rendered*** homeless by the earthquake.

➢ Your action has ***rendered*** our contract invalid.

4. **lest** /lest/ *conj*. in order to prevent something from happening 免得，以免

➢ Every item you buy at the supermarket is being tracked and potentially data-mined, ***lest*** there be a combination of goods in your basket that the authorities don't like. (Para. 3)

➢ He gripped his brother's arm ***lest*** he be trampled by the mob.

5. **invoke** /ɪnˈvəʊk/ *v*. to mention a person, a theory, an example, etc. to support your opinions or ideas, or as a reason for something 提及，援引（某人、某理论、实例等作为支持）

➢ In the mid-1970s, the Panopticon prison design was ***invoked*** by French philosopher Michel Foucault as metaphor for modern "disciplinary" societies and their pervasive inclination to observe and normalize. (Para. 6)

➢ She ***invoked*** several eminent scholars to back up her argument.

6. **pervasive** /pəˈveɪsɪv/ *adj*. existing in all parts of a place or thing; spreading gradually to affect all parts of a place or thing 遍布的，充斥各处的，弥漫的

➢ In the mid-1970s, the Panopticon prison design was invoked by French philosopher Michel Foucault as metaphor for modern "disciplinary" societies and their ***pervasive*** inclination to observe and normalize. (Para. 6)

➢ A sense of social change is ***pervasive*** in her novels.

7. **proliferation** /prəˌlɪfəˈreɪʃn/ *n*. the sudden increase in the number or amount of something; a large number of a particular thing 激增，涌现，增殖，大量的事物

➢ After Brin, Jensen and Draffan, among others, have demonstrated how our society is being pushed towards a panopticon-like state, thanks to the *proliferation* of surveillance technologies. (Para. 7)

➢ Nuclear *proliferation* has returned to center stage in international affairs.

8. omniscient /ɒmˈnɪsiənt/ *adj*. knowing everything 无所不知的，全知全能的，博闻广识的

➢ By comforting a form of government characterized by *omniscient* surveillance and mechanical law enforcement, the Internet of Things would make that humans will lose control over sensing and actuating objects. (Para. 8)

➢ The novel has an *omniscient* narrator.

9. granular /ˈɡrænjələ(r)/ *adj*. consisting of small granules; looking or feeling like a collection of granules 由颗粒构成的，含颗粒的，似颗粒状的

➢ Using various technologies, such as GPS-enabled smartphones, we are beginning to measure ourselves in *granular* detail—how long we sleep, where we drive, what we breathe, what we eat, how we spend our time. (Para. 9)

➢ We show that the operating principle is the ability of *granular* materials to transition between an unjammed, deformable state and a jammed state with solid-like rigidity.

10. contemplate /ˈkɒntəmpleɪt/ *v*. to think deeply about something for a long time 深思熟虑，沉思，苦思冥想

➢ We feel it as a moral obligation to *contemplate* a bright scenario, one in which the Internet of Things will be designed to develop new usages that will empower individuals, not control them. (Para. 10)

➢ She lay in bed, *contemplating*.

➢ That makes it difficult to *contemplate* the idea that the present policy may not be sustainable.

重点短语

1. remind sb. of sb. /sth.: to make somebody remember or think about the other person, place, thing, etc. because they are similar in some way 使想起(类似的人、地方、事物等)

➢ A few days following that publication, I had an interesting e-mail exchange with Rob van Kranenburg on the concept of Panopticon, and this *reminded* me *of* his book on the Internet of Things, in which ... (Para. 2)

➢ You *remind* me *of* your father when you say that.

2. in place of sb. /sth. in sb. 's/sth. 's place: instead of somebody/something 代替，顶替

➢ ... to expand on the vision of a City of Trust that would emerge *in place of* a City of Control. (Para. 2)

➢ You can use milk *in place of* cream in this recipe.

➢ He was unable to come to the ceremony, but he sent his son to accept the award *in*

his place.

3. a nest of：一套

Nest：a group or set of similar things that are made to fit inside each other(套叠在一起的)一套物件

➢ In our future cities (...) instead of ***a nest of*** cameras atop each lamppost, lies a near invisible network of wireless frequencies ... (Para.3)

➢ There was ***a nest of*** field mice in the back of the car.

4. it transpires (that)：It is known or has been shown to be true. 公开，透露，为人所知

➢ ... which ***it transpires*** were rather poor at fighting crime anyway. (Para.3)

➢ ***It transpired that*** the gang had had a contact inside the bank.

➢ This story, ***it*** later ***transpired***, was untrue.

5. given (that)：taking (something) into account; when you consider something 考虑到，鉴于

➢ However, ***given*** our knowledge and practical experience of history, the drivers for control and surveillance in governance systems and ... (Para.12)

➢ ***Given*** her interest in children, teaching seems the right job for her.

6. be endowed with sth.：to naturally have a particular feature, quality, etc. 天生赋有，生来具有(某种特性、品质等)

➢ Said differently, what could be the metaphor of a free society where individuals ***are endowed with*** the capability to exploit their talents and realize their dreams ... (Para.13)

➢ She ***was endowed with*** intelligence and wit.

难句解析

1. Security is the defining issue for those who can afford it, but also for those that cannot. (Para.3)

Paraphrase: For people who can or cannot pay for security, security itself is the decisive topic of problem.

解析：句中 but also 是 not only ... but also ...结构的省略用法，即 but also 单独出现，前面不用 not only。举例如下：

➢ It depends on your point of view, ***but also*** on where you live.

➢ Entering WTO is not only an opportunity, ***but also*** a challenge for China.

➢ The article, based on a lengthy interview with Kidd, ***but also*** on discussions with other figures in Joyce and general editorial scholarship, contained the essentials of the row which was then inevitable.

翻译：安全性对于能负担起和不能负担起的人们来说都是决定性因素。

2. If we accept that vision of modern society, it comes to mind that the Internet of Things holds the potential of pushing the limits far beyond what has been until now

state of the art of such technologies (Para. 7)

Paraphrase: If we believe that the modern society will be panopticon-like, we will think of the future that the Internet of Things is capable to develop the most advanced technologies to a much higher level.

解析：本句前半句是 if 引导的条件状语从句，复合句的主句是 it comes to mind，其中 it 是形式主语，真正的主语是 that 引导的从句。举例如下：

➢ ***It*** is quite certain ***that*** he will be at the meeting.

➢ ***It*** is a pity ***that*** you should have to leave.

➢ ***It*** is suggested ***that*** the work should be done with great care.

翻译：如果我们接受现代社会的那种景象，那么浮现在脑海的就是物联网拥有远远突破迄今为止现有高科技水平的潜力。

3. The pressure to adopt these technologies springs from the current political discourse as nations struggle to confront ill-defined threats. (Para. 7)

Paraphrase: When each nation is trying to deal with unclear threats, the present opinions in the political field become the stress for us to use these technologies.

解析：本句是 as 引导的伴随状语从句，强调主句和从句中的动作或状态同时发生，从句可放在主句前，也可放在主句后。举例如下：

➢ ***As*** the production increased by 20 percent, we have had another good harvest year.

➢ The fog dispersed ***as*** the sun rose.

➢ ***As*** computers spread into all sorts of other products, such specialized silicon will be very useful.

翻译：当各国都在努力应对不明确的威胁时，采用这些技术的压力来自当前的政治舆论。

4. ... data is wirelessly uploaded to the Web so that they can monitor their activity and compare it with that of their friends. (Para. 9)

Paraphrase: ... data is transmitted to the Internet through radio waves, so people can check their activity and compare it with their friends' activity.

解析：本句是 so that 引导的结果状语从句，难点是"that of their friends"中 that 的用法，此处的 that 用于引入有关上文已提及的某事物的更多信息，而避免重复提及相关名词。举例如下：

➢ A recession like ***that*** of 1973 - 1974 could put one in ten American companies into bankruptcy.

➢ The extent of the improvements in military receivers' capability resulting from this option would be somewhat greater than ***that*** from Option 1 and could be realized just as quickly.

➢ Indoor pollution falls into two categories, ***that*** which we can see or smell, and pollution which is invisible and produces no odour.

翻译：数据被无线上传到网上，这样他们就可以监控自己的活动，并将其与朋友的活动进行比较。

5. The Internet of Things is not destined to be "The Matrix"! (Para. 12)

Paraphrase: The future of the Internet of Things has been decided or planned beforehand to be the situation in the movie "The Matrix".

解析：本句的难点是"The Matrix"，即《黑客帝国》，是华纳兄弟影片公司 1999 年的一部动作、科幻电影，影片由安迪·沃卓斯基和拉娜·沃卓斯基共同担任导演及编剧，基努·李维斯、凯瑞·安·莫斯和劳伦斯·菲什伯恩等联袂出演。电影于 1999 年 3 月 31 日在美国上映。影片讲述一名年轻的网络黑客尼奥发现看似正常的现实世界，实际上是由一个名为"矩阵"的计算机人工智能系统控制的。尼奥在一名神秘女郎崔妮蒂的引导下见到了黑客组织的首领墨菲斯，三人走上了抗争矩阵的征途。本句用"The Matrix"是借用影片来指代物联网的发展不是注定就会成为《黑客帝国》中人类被人工智能和机器人控制的情况。

翻译：物联网并非注定会成为《黑客帝国》电影中的样子。

写作技巧

Parallel Structure

Overview

Parallelism is a grammatical term for arranging words of identical or equivalent syntactical constructions in corresponding clauses, phrases, lists, etc. Parallel structure, also called parallelism, means using the same grammatical structure for ideas that are similar or of equal importance. Basically, similar ideas should be in similar form. Parallel structure is most often used at the word, phrase, and clause levels. It is essential to accurate grammatical structure, as it improves coherence and consistency. All good writers understand the importance of parallelism and are mindful of it when constructing their sentences. The usual way to join parallel structures is with the use of coordinating conjunctions such as "and" "or" "but" "yet" "so", etc.

For *words*, nouns are balanced with nouns, adjectives with adjectives, verbs with verbs, gerunds with gerunds, and so on.

For *phrases*, prepositional phrases are balanced with prepositional phrases, infinitive phrases with infinitive phrases, and gerund phrases with gerund phrases.

For *clauses*, simple sentences with simple sentences, dependent clauses with dependent clauses, and so on. ??

Here are some examples:

➢ **Incorrect**: Your new training program was *stimulating* and a *challenge*.
 Correct: Your new training program was *stimulating* and *challenging*.

➢ **Incorrect**: I attended *a conference*, *weddings*, and *a bar mitzvah* last summer.

Correct: I attended *a conference*, *three weddings*, and *a bar mitzvah* last summer.

- **Incorrect**: Please *place the leftover chicken on the counter* or *you can put it in the refrigerator*.

  Correct: Please place the leftover chicken *on the counter* or *in the refrigerator*.
- **Incorrect**: The room was *comfortable*, *airy*, and *it was not dirty*.

  Correct: The room was *comfortable*, *airy*, and *clean*.
- **Incorrect**: My parents did not approve of *my actions* or *what I said*.

  Correct: My parents did not approve of *what I did* nor *what I said*.

NOTE: Parallelism is especially important in displayed enumerations.

Here are three versions of an article introduction:

- **Poor**: This article will discuss:
  1. How to deal with corporate politics.
  2. Coping with stressful situations.
  3. What the role of the manager should be in the community.
- **Better**: This article will discuss:
  1. Ways to deal with corporate politics.
  2. Techniques of coping with stressful situations.
  3. The role of the manager in the community.
- **Or**: This article will tell managers how to:
  1. Deal with corporate politics.
  2. Cope with stressful situations.
  3. Function in the community

Sample Sentence Analysis

- **Sample Sentences**

1. The Panopticon is used as a metaphor for describing a "surveillance society" where technology is **extensively and routinely** used to track and record human activities and movements in ways which are invisible to ordinary people as they are watched and monitored. (Para. 1)
2. **Everything** you buy, **every person** you meet, **every move** you make. (Para. 3)
3. Using various technologies, such as GPS-enabled smartphones, we are beginning to measure ourselves in granular detail—**how long we sleep**, **where we drive**, **what we breathe**, **what we eat**, **how we spend our time**. (Para. 9)
4. A time could come when the trillions of smart objects interacting with people in a "brave new world"—from gizmos to spimes to biots, according to Bruce Sterling's typology—will **bring about their own revolution**, **rise up in revolt**, **herd the human race into Panopticon prisons**, **and punish those humans** least able to respect their laws and jargon and to rid themselves of the specifically human

characteristics which hold them at a distance from the centre of social activity. (Para. 7)

5. **Let's imagine** if the data from all social networks were combined with all the location data, call and SMS records for all mobile phones; then **let's imagine** combining all that data with data from retailer databases, credit agencies, voter registration records, real estate transactions, and so on. (Para. 8)

➢ **Structure Analysis**

Sentence 1

Parallel structure is shown in pairs, like "**extensively** and **routinely**" "**track** and **record**" "**watched** and **monitored**", which look clear and sound pleasant.

Sentence 2

Three examples are set to illustrate how people are watched following a pattern of pronouns or noun phrases attached with "you do" clause.

Sentence 3

To demonstrate how our life is penetrated by measurement, five noun clauses are listed neatly, led by subordinate correlatives like how, where and what.

Sentence 4

This sentence adopts verb phrases like "*bring about their own revolution*" "*rise up in revolt*" to maintain parallel.

In Line 3 & 4, four verb phrases (as shown in bold letters) are strung together to describe what small objects will do. These four consecutive parallel actions create an intense and horrifying effect.

Sentence 5

This sentence uses two imperative sentences (祈使句) to make parallel structures, and the structure used here is "*Let's imagine* ...".

This sentence is cut into two halves by a semicolon. Each half starts with "Let's imagine ..." to drive readers to imagine the consequences when humans lose control.

Get started on your own

Directions: 1. Read the text carefully and write an analysis of sentences with parallel structures.

2. Can you find some other ways to make parallel structures? What are they?

篇章分析

This article talks about the future society with the development of technology, especially IoT. At the very beginning, the author uses Liu Yongmou's Chinese article published in the "Council on the Internet of Things" website to tell us what is "surveillance society" and the metaphor **panopticon** involved. Then, in the second and the third paragraph, the author mentions his communication with Rob van Kranenburg on the concept of Panopticon and describes the surveillance state in future cities: the state of a city of Trust and a city of Control. Items concerned in the tale of these two cities are: cameras, radio frequency, tagged objects and spaces, notions of public and private, security issue, access to parts of the city, tracked and data-mined items people buy, etc. From Para. 4 to Para. 7, the definition of Panopticon designed by Jeremy Bentham is introduced together with the essential feature of Bentham's design and Michel Foucault's claim about all hierarchical structures. Following Foucault, Jensen and Draffan, demonstrate the society is being pushed towards a panopticon-like state with the development of technology. A new time with threats is coming. The next two paragraphs describe the dangers and threats of IoT: fragments of data all together creating a powerful Panopticon society. Finally, we find from Para. 10 to Para. 13, the author is not pessimistic but calls for the contemplation of a bright scenario. We can also see from the e-mail with Rob van Kranenburg, the question "what could be the metaphor of a free society, the City of Trust" is proposed to provoke thought.

We visualize the text structure by means of a mind map.

Panopticon as a Metaphor of the Internet of Things

—Why Not? But If It Were the Opposite?

- **Panopticon and the "surveillance society" (Paras. 1 – 3)**
  - Introduction (Para. 1)
  - E-mail exchange with Rob van Kranenburg (Para. 2)
  - Description of the surveillance state in the future cities (Para. 3)
- **Panopticon and IoT (Paras. 4 – 7)**
  - Definition of Panopticon by Jeremy Bentham (Para. 4)
  - Essential feature of Bentham's design (Para. 5)
  - Michel Foucault's claim (Para. 6)
  - A new time with IoT and threats (Para. 7)
- **Threats and its source (Paras. 8 – 9)**
  - Fragments of data in a whole (Para. 8)
  - Privacy leakage from granular details (Para. 9)
- **The optimistic discussion and the question proposed (Paras. 10 – 13)**
  - E-mail discussion (Para. 10)
  - The optimistic view (Paras. 11 – 12)
  - Thoughts about a free society (Para. 13)

课堂提问

➢ What do you know about IoT?

- Can you describe the City of Control? (Para. 3)
- What is the essential feature of Bentham's design? (Para. 5)
- Is the Panopticon the metaphor of what we want for the Internet of Things? (Para. 10)
- What will be the opposite concept for the freedom society? (Para. 13)

教学建议

This article introduces the development of technology and its influence on the future society. The author refers to several famous persons including philosophers, scholars and science fiction writers to further explain his idea. If students know more about these famous persons and their related articles, they will understand the text much thoroughly. This article is not difficult, but there are many technical terms, so students are suggested to be able to understand and accumulate these technical terms for further use. Meanwhile, students should also grasp the writing skills in this article and use them on their own.

B. 课堂讨论模块

学习时间

2 hours

讨论内容

- To discuss the benefits and troubles that IoT brings us.
- To use the words and expressions learned to discuss issues about IoT.
- To use one's professional knowledge to predict the future of IoT.

教学方法

heuristic teaching; group discussion; class presentation

组织形式

- Let each group of students present a PPT about IoT.
- Discuss their expectation of the future society in groups and then present their group's idea after discussion.

参考问题

- Can you describe Panopticon and its usage as a metaphor of IoT in the future society in your own words?
- What are the benefits and troubles that IoT brings us?
- What do you think is the future society with technology?

课后练习

Refer to the exercises in Unit Four of the textbook.

练习答案

Part 1 Reading Comprehension

1. **Directions**：Do the following statements agree with the information given in the reading passage? In blanks 1)－5)，choose

   TRUE if the statement agrees with the information.

   FALSE if the statement contradicts the information.

   NOT GIVEN if there is no such information in the statement.

   1) F (Para.10) 2) T (Para.3) 3) F (Para.3) 4) NG (Para.1) 5) T (Para.7)

2. **Directions**：Paraphrase the following sentences.

   1) Whether for people who can or cannot pay for security，security itself is a decisive subject.

   2) The current government's political belief leads to the use of these technologies to govern human behavior because nations are trying to cope with uncertain threat.

   3) As time goes by，people increasingly believe that we live in a dangerous world and the entire society increasingly longs for safety.

   4) People themselves will increasingly manipulate surveillance technologies，that's to say，the real "threat" may stem from people themselves.

   5) A pessimistic Panopticon situation may not occur because the future has not been set yet.

Part 2 Words and Expressions

3. **Directions**：Choose proper words from the following word bank，and fill in blanks in their right forms.

   1) proliferate 2) lest 3) surveillant 4) pervasive 5) illegitimate
   6) ubiquitous 7) evokes 8) invoke 9) enslaved 10) omniscient

Part 3 Translation

4. **Directions**：Translate the following sentences from the reading passage into Chinese.

   1) 在未来城市中……取代灯柱上诸多摄像头的是隐形的无线频率网络。在这个网络上，其中几乎任何事物、空间（就像易趣上任何一件物品或是易捷上所有航班的票价信息一样）都可轻而易举被找到、监控、发现并记录。

   2) 这一目标在当时技术条件限制下极难实现，但随着20世纪的科技发展，尤其是闭路电视摄像机的出现，接近于边沁(Bentham)这一愿景的实现便成为可能。

   3) 当数以万亿的智能对象与人们在"勇敢的新世界"中交互之时，一个时代将会到来，从布鲁斯·斯特林(Bruce Sterling)类型学中提到的小玩意到远程跟踪物再到生物类型，都将发起它们自己的革命，在反抗中崛起，驱使人类进入圆形监狱，惩罚那些最不能尊重他们法律和行话的人，惩罚那些最不能摆脱人类特征的人，因为这特征会让他们无法接近社会活动中心。

4）物联网给以全方位监控和机械执法为特征的政府模式提供安抚（以缓解其不安全感），这使人类失去对感知和驱动设备的控制。

5）换句话说，在一个自由社会里，个人被赋予了发挥才能和实现梦想的能力，社会团体团结一致，社会组织遵守道德。这样的自由社会可以比喻为什么呢？

Part 4　Sentence Structure

5. **Directions**: Combine the following sentences in each group into a complex sentence.

1）California's growth rate dropped during the 1970's, to 18.5 percent—little more than two thirds the 1960's growth figure and considerably below that of other Western states.

2）Unlike most of the world's volcanoes, they are not always found at the boundaries of the great drifting plates that make up the earth's surface.

3）At the same time, the American Law Institute—a group of judges, lawyers, and academics whose recommendations carry substantial weight—issued new guidelines for tort law stating that companies need not warn customers of obvious dangers or bombard them with a lengthy list of possible ones.

4）Problems in dispute can be settled through teleconferencing without the participants leaving their homes and/or jobs to travel to a distant conference site.

5）Dependence is marked first by an increased tolerance, with more and more of the substance required to produce the desired effect, and then by the appearance of unpleasant withdrawal symptoms when the substance is discontinued.

Part 5　Academic Writing Skills

6. **Directions**: Read the following material and analyze how the paragraphs are developed logically and coherently.

Broadly speaking, there are two approaches to constructing protocols for secure computation. Generic protocols can be used to evaluate arbitrary functions, given a description of the function as a circuit; special-purpose protocols are tailored to specific functions of interest. Yao's "garbled circuit" approach [21] (extended in [8] to handle malicious adversaries) gives a generic protocol for secure two-party computation. In recent years several implementations and improvements of Yao's garbled circuit protocol have been shown [16, 10, 14, 15, 19, 18]. Regardless of any improvements, however, a fundamental limitation of **this** approach is that the garbled circuit has size linear in the size of the circuit being computed.

More efficient, special-purpose protocols have been developed for several functionalities of interest. Several efficient protocols for keyword search are known [4, 12, 9, 3]; there also exist efficient protocols for pattern matching [20, 9, 6] but, as discussed previously, **these** protocols do not seem to extend to more complex functionalities such as the **ones** we consider **here**. While several researchers have also investigated specific problems related to DNA matching [2,20,11,5], none of **these** works seem to apply to **our** specific problem. Finally, we also mention recent work on oblivious evaluation of finite automata [20,5,6]. Applying **such** protocols directly to **our** setting seems to yield less efficient protocols. Moreover, **our** approach allows for the computation of functions that cannot be computed by finite automata.

7. **Directions**: Apart from grammatical mistakes, the following paragraph also lacks coherence. Try to polish the paragraph.

ReLU [Nair and Hinton, 2010], a widely-used activation function, is essentially a neuron with a rectified unit. **While** in the majority of the deep convolutional neural networks, such as VGGs [Simonyan and Zisserman, 2014], ResNets [He et al., 2016a], and DenseNets [Huang et al., 2017], ReLU is used with desirable results, the community is **still** devoted to developing new activation functions with performance **better than** ReLU ([Maas et al., 2013], [Agostinelli et al., 2014], [He et al., 2015], [Hendrycks and Gimpel, 2016], [Qiu and Cai, 2017], [Elfwing et al., 2017]). **However**, most of **those** newly-developed activation functions do not fare well in terms of performance. Ramachandran et al. (2017) and Xu et al. (2015) systematically investigated the performance of different types of rectified activation functions in convolutional neural networks, and the investigation showed the inconsistent performance improvements of these new activation functions across different models and datasets. **Therefore**, ReLU is **still** the most favorable activation function in the neural network community due to its simplicity, effectiveness, and generalization.

Unit Five Artificial Intelligence

Section A Franken-Algorithms: The Deadly Consequences of Unpredictable Code

文章主旨

This article starts with a car accident which draws our enormous attention to self-driving vehicles, and its supporting technology—artificial intelligence (AI). The death of a woman hit by a self-driving car highlights an unfolding technological crisis, as code piled on code creates "a universe no one fully understands". Then the author talks about "What is an algorithm?" In this part, the article illustrates the historical change of the algorithm's meanings, from a simple rule to recipes for treating data, to any large, complex decision-making software system, or any means of taking an array of input of data and assessing it quickly, to independent entities with lives of their own, to algorithms doing what they've been programmed to do, to human-like artificial general intelligence, or AGI. Finally, this article presents the problem, that is, once an algorithm is learning, we no longer know to any degree of certainty what its rules and parameters are. The algorithms probably become unstable and unpredictable.

教学目标

- To have a thorough understanding of the text.
- To learn how to express ideas with complicated sentences.
- To be able to use the knowledge learned to discuss issues about algorithms, AI, etc.
- To drill students how to acquire the central meanings of paragraphs.

学习时间

4 hours (2 hours for the text; 2 hours for discussion)

A. 课堂讲授模块

预习要求

- To learn and recite the new words.
- To grasp the main idea of the text after reading.
- To search for materials related to AI.

学习时间

2 hours

教学方法

heuristic teaching; project-based teaching; task-driven teaching; group discussion; self-study and peer learning

组织形式

- Let the students work in groups to discuss the text structure and its main idea based on fast reading, and to draw a simple mind-map as well.
- Summarize key technical terms, words and phrases, and sentence patterns in articles involving such technologies as light-emitting lidar sensors, algorithm, code, AI, AGI, etc.
- Let the students discuss in groups the learning gains based on their fields of research, and a presentation is expected.
- Analyze the complex sentences and technical issues. Spare some time to respond to any questions from the students.

背景知识

1. Frankenstein

Frankenstein, the title character in Mary Wollstonecraft Shelley's novel *Frankenstein*, is the prototypical "mad scientist" who creates a monster by which he is eventually killed. The name Frankenstein has become popularly attached to the creature itself, who has become the best-known monster in the history of motion pictures.

Shelley's novel, *Frankenstein*, or, *the Modern Prometheus* (1818), is a combination of Gothic horror story and science fiction. The book tells the story of Victor Frankenstein, a Swiss student of natural science who creates an artificial man from pieces of corpses and brings his creature to life. Though it initially seeks affection, the monster inspires loathing in everyone who meets it. Lonely and miserable, the monster turns upon its creator, who eventually loses his life.

2. Lidar vs. RADAR

Every month new advanced driver-assistance systems (ADAS) and other cutting-edge self-driving innovations hit the automobile market. Apart from machine learning, Internet of Things (IoT), and the cloud, two technologies namely LIDAR (Light Detection and Ranging) and RADAR (Radio Detection and Ranging) seem to be leading the way in the development of advanced self-driving vehicles.

Lidar (/ˈlaɪdɑːr/, called LIDAR, LiDAR, and LADAR) is a surveying method that measures distance to a target by illuminating the target with laser light and measuring the reflected light with a sensor. Differences in laser return times and wavelengths can then be used to make digital 3D representations of the target.

The Lidar instrument emits rapid laser signals, sometimes up to 150,000 pulses per second. The signals bounce back from the obstacles. The sensor positioned on the instrument measures the amount of time it takes for each pulse to bounce back. Thus, the instrument can calculate the distance between itself and the obstacle with accuracy. It can also detect the exact size of the object. Lidar is commonly used to make high-resolution maps.

The RADAR system works in much the same way as the Lidar, with the only difference being that it uses radio waves instead of laser. In the RADAR instrument, the antenna doubles up as a radar receiver as well as a transmitter. However, radio waves have less absorption compared to the light waves when contacting objects. Thus, they can work over a relatively long distance. The most well-known use of RADAR technology is for military purposes. Airplanes and battleships are often equipped with RADAR to measure altitude and detect other transport devices and objects in the vicinity.

Most autonomous vehicle manufacturers including Google, Uber, and Toyota rely heavily on the Lidar systems to navigate the vehicle. The Lidar sensors are often used to generate detailed maps of the immediate surroundings such as pedestrians, speed breakers, dividers, and other vehicles. Its ability to create a three-dimensional image is one of the reasons why most automakers are keenly interested in developing this technology with the sole exception of the famous automaker Tesla. Tesla's self-driving cars rely on RADAR technology as the primary sensor.

High-end Lidar sensors can identify the details of a few centimeters at more than 100 meters. For example, Waymo's Lidar system not only detects pedestrians but it can also tell which direction they're facing. Thus, the autonomous vehicle can accurately predict where the pedestrian will walk. The high-level of accuracy also allows it to see details such as a cyclist waving to let you pass, two football fields away while driving at full speed with incredible accuracy. Waymo has also managed to cut the price of Lidar sensors by almost 90% in the recent years. A single unit with a price tag of $75,000 a few years ago will now cost just $7,500, making this technology affordable.

3. Ellen Ullman

Ellen Ullman (born on Jun 13, 1949, graduated from Cornell University) is an American computer programmer and author. She has written novels as well as articles for various publications, including *Harper's Magazine*, *Wired*, *The New York Times* and *Salon*. She owned a consulting firm and worked as technology commentator for NPR's All Things Considered. Her essays and novels analyze the human side of the world of computer programming. Her breakthrough book was non-fiction: *Close to the Machine: Technophilia and Its Discontents*.

Banner in the Sky written by Ellen Ullman was first published in 1954.

She began working professionally in 1978 as a programmer of EDI applications and graphical user interfaces that preceded Microsoft Windows.

In 1995 she wrote an essay, *Out of Time: Reflections on the Programming Life*.

Close to the Machine: Technophilia and Its Discontents written by Ellen Ullman was first published in 1997.

Life in Code: A Personal History of Technology written by Ellen Ullman was first published on August 08,2017.

4. Utopian

Utopia, an ideal commonwealth whose inhabitants exist under seemingly perfect conditions. Hence, utopian and utopianism are words used to denote visionary reform that tends to be impossibly idealistic.

The word first occurred in Sir Thomas More's *Utopia*, published in Latin as "Libellus ... de optimo reipublicae statu, deque nova insula Utopia" (1516; "Concerning the highest state of the republic and the new island Utopia"); it was compounded by More from the Greek words for "not" (ou) and "place" (topos) and thus meant "nowhere." During his embassy to Flanders in 1515, More wrote *Book* Ⅱ *of Utopia*, describing a pagan and communist city-state in which the institutions and policies were entirely governed by reason. The order and dignity of such a state was intended to provide a notable contrast with the unreasonable polity of Christian Europe, divided by self-interest and greed for power and riches, which More then described in Book Ⅰ, written in England in 1516. The description of *Utopia* is put in the mouth of a mysterious traveler, Raphael Hythloday, in support of his argument that communism is the only cure against egoism in private and public life. More, in the dialogue, speaks in favour of mitigation of evil rather than cure, human nature being fallible. The reader is thus left guessing as to which parts of the brilliant jeu d'esprit are seriously intended and which are mere paradox.

5. Sales pitch

In selling technique, a sales presentation or sales pitch is a line of talk that attempts to persuade someone or something, with a planned sales presentation strategy of a product or service designed to initiate and close a sale of the product or service. In short, sales pitch is a speech that is given in order to persuade someone to buy something.

A good sales pitch also has a structure that makes it easy for the buyer to follow what you're presenting. One of the more common structures used in sales presentations is that of articulating what the buyer's problem is; presenting a potential solution to that problem; and finally agreeing to a next step with the buyer.

5 Best Cinematic Sales Pitches:

➢ Boiler Room(抢钱大作战)
➢ Tommy Boy(乌龙兄弟)
➢ Glengary Glen Ross(大亨游戏)
➢ The Music Man (first 3 minutes)(欢乐音乐妙无限)
➢ Pursuit of Happiness(当幸福来敲门)

Any successful sales pitch can benefit from telling the story of your brand and product. And when you do this effectively, you will create a stronger connection between you and your buyers. This connection is often based on the fact that they can relate to your brand on a personal level, giving them even more reasons to buy.

6. Arcade games

An arcade game is a game machine typically found in public places like malls, restaurants and amusement arcades, and is usually coin operated. Arcade games are usually video games, pinball machines or electromechanical games. The late 1970s and throughout the 1980s was the golden age of the arcade games. They enjoyed some relative popularity even during the early 1990s. The popularity of this platform slowly declined, however, as console and PC games came into prominence.

7. Google's DeepMind

With the boom in artificial intelligence (AI) affecting virtually every industry, there has been an explosion in the research and development of machine learning, a subfield of AI. And, perhaps, no company better illustrates what machine learning is capable of than Google's DeepMind.

Founded in London in 2010 by Demis Hassabis, Shane Legg, and Mustafa Suleyman, DeepMind has developed machine learning systems that uses deep neural networks, reinforcement learning, and systems neuroscience-inspired models. The startup was purchased in January 2014 by Google for a reported 400 million, with Hassabis remaining CEO of DeepMind.

➢ **What is DeepMind**? Google DeepMind is a machine learning system that uses algorithms based on deep neural networks and reinforcement learning to train on massive datasets to be able to predict outcomes.
➢ **Why does DeepMind matter**? Google DeepMind is a prominent example of machine

learning that illustrates what advanced AI is capable of.

- **Who does DeepMind affect?** Anyone from businesses to computer scientists to engineers to end-users will be impacted by machine learning. The principles used by DeepMind can be applied to businesses that want to improve efficiency and gamers who want to learn how to master certain games, like Go.
- **When is DeepMind happening?** Google DeepMind came into the public eye in October 2015 when it beat the European champion of Go, marking a breakthrough in artificial intelligence that came a decade earlier than many experts predicted.
- **How can I take advantage of DeepMind?** While Google isn't sharing all the details of its machine learning secrets, much of its code is open source, and it has also shared the code of its software called TensorFlow, a deep learning engine. DeepMind also publishes many academic papers about its work online.

8. Cuttlefish & Aphid

Cephalopod intelligence（头足类动物智能）is a measure of the cognitive ability of the cephalopod class of molluscs（软体动物）. Intelligence is generally defined as the process of acquiring, storing in memory, retrieving, combining, comparing, and using in new contexts information and conceptual skills. Though these criteria are difficult to measure in nonhuman animals, cephalopods seem to be exceptionally intelligent invertebrates（无脊椎动物）. The study of cephalopod intelligence also has an important comparative aspect in the broader understanding of animal cognition because it relies on a nervous system fundamentally different from that of vertebrates. In particular, the Coleoidea subclass（**cuttlefish 乌贼**, squid 鱿鱼, and octopuses 章鱼）is thought to be the most intelligent invertebrates and an important example of advanced cognitive evolution in animals, though nautilus（鹦鹉螺）intelligence is also a subject of growing interest among zoologists.

Aphid（蚜虫）,（family Aphididae 蚜科）, also called plant louse, greenfly, or ant cow, any of a group of sap-sucking, soft-bodied insects（order Homoptera 同翅目）that are about the size of a pinhead, most species of which have a pair of tubelike projections（cornicles 腹管）on the abdomen. Aphids can be serious plant pests and may stunt plant growth, produce plant galls, transmit plant virus diseases, and cause the deformation of leaves, buds, and flowers.

9. Transfer learning

Transfer learning（迁移学习）is the dependency of human conduct, learning, or performance on prior experience. The notion was originally introduced as transfer of practice by Edward Thorndike and Robert S. Woodworth. They explored how individuals would transfer learning in one context to another similar context—or how "improvement in one mental function" could influence a related one. Their theory implied that transfer of learning depends on how similar the learning task and transfer tasks are, or where "identical elements are concerned in the influencing and influenced function", now known as the identical element theory.

Transfer learning is a machine learning method where a model developed for a task is reused as the starting point for a model on a second task.

It is a popular approach in deep learning where pre-trained models are used as the starting point on computer vision and natural language processing tasks given the vast compute and time resources required to develop neural network models on these problems and from the huge jumps in skill that they provide on related problems.

重点词汇

1. **dread** /dred/ *v*. be afraid or scared of; be frightened of 畏惧，害怕
   - The 18th of March 2018, was the day tech insiders had been ***dreading***. (Para. 1)
   - Death is not only a biological threat, and a very permanent one, but it is also a psychological threat that we ***dread***.
2. **stationary** /ˈsteɪʃ(ə)n(ə)rɪ/ *adj*. something that is stationary is not moving 静止不动的
   - But objects in roads seldom remain ***stationary*** ... (Para. 1)
   - ***Stationary*** cars in traffic jams cause a great deal of pollution.
3. **crawl** /krɔːl/ *v*. to search the Internet for hosts, Web pages or blogs 爬取(SYN) spider, browse
   - ... so more algorithms ***crawled*** a database of recognizable mechanical and biological entities ... (Para. 1)
   - Once the ***crawl***, parse and index, and search components have started running, you need to search some keywords in the search application to make sure some query log data is being generated.
4. **bar** /bɑː/ *n*. If someone is barred from a place or from doing something, they are officially forbidden to go there or to do it. 禁止 [usu. passive]
   - ***Barred*** from taking evasive action on its own, the computer abruptly handed control back to its human master, but the master wasn't paying attention. (Para. 2)
   - Amnesty workers have been ***barred*** from the country since 1982.
5. **fervidly** /ˈfəːvidli/ *adv*. with passionate fervor 热情，热烈(SYN) fierily, fervently, ardently
   - Few subjects are more constantly or ***fervidly*** discussed right now than algorithms. (Para. 6)
   - Since long, many theorists have ***fervidly*** studied this theme, and put forward a lot of valuable viewpoints.

6. **portentous** /pɔːˈtentəs/ *adj*. 1) If someone's way of speaking, writing, or behaving is portentous, they speak, write, or behave more seriously than necessary because they want to impress other people. 自命不凡的，装腔作势的[正式] 2) Something that is portentous is important in indicating or affecting future events. 预示未来的，影响重大的[正式]

  ➢ Recent years have seen a more ***portentous*** and ambiguous meaning emerge ... (Para. 7)

  ➢ Such a ***portentous*** and mysterious monster roused all my curiosity.

7. **nuanced** /ˈnjuːɑːnst/ *adj*. A nuance is a small difference in sound, feeling, appearance, or meaning. （声音、感觉、外貌或意义等方面的）细微差别（SYN） delicate, subtle, refined

  ➢ Only since 2016 has a more ***nuanced*** consideration of our new algorithmic reality begun to take shape. (Para. 8)

  ➢ His view of Europe, too, is more ***nuanced*** than some might expect.

8. **detachment** /dɪˈtætʃm(ə)nt/ *n*. Detachment is the feeling that you have of not being personally involved in something or of having no emotional interest in it. 客观，超然

  ➢ Corporations like Facebook and Google have sold and defended their algorithms on the promise of objectivity, an ability to weigh a set of conditions with mathematical ***detachment*** and absence of fuzzy emotion. (Para. 8)

  ➢ If you can do so once in a while, you will be able to manifest more and more emotional and mental ***detachment***, which will help you on your road to success and achieving your goals and ambitions.

9. **eradicate** /ɪˈrædɪkeɪt/ *v*. To eradicate something means to get rid of it completely. 根除

  ➢ In her 2016 book *Weapons of Math Destruction*, Cathy O'Neil, a former math prodigy who left Wall Street to teach and write and run the excellent mathbabe blog, demonstrated beyond question that, far from ***eradicating*** human biases, algorithms could magnify and entrench them. (Para. 9)

  ➢ They are already battling to ***eradicate*** illnesses such as malaria and tetanus(疟疾、破伤风).

10. **underpinning** /ˈʌndəpɪnɪŋ/ *n*. If one thing underpins another, it helps the other thing to continue or succeed by supporting and strengthening it. 基础，支柱，支撑

  ➢ A skilled coder can in principle examine and challenge their ***underpinnings***. (Para. 11)

  ➢ It's threatening the very ***underpinnings*** of our society.

11. **laud** /lɔːd/ *v*. If people laud someone, they praise and admire them. 嘉许，称赞

  ➢ To put this into perspective, Google's DeepMind division has been justly ***lauded*** for creating a program capable of mastering arcade games, starting with nothing more than an instruction to aim for the highest possible score. (Para.12)

➢ Dickens was ***lauded*** for his social and moral sensitivity.

12. **inured** /iˈnjuəd/ *adj*. If you are inured to something unpleasant, you have become used to it so that it no longer affects you. 习以为常的

 ➢ Where the "dumb" fixed algorithms—complex, opaque and ***inured*** to real time monitoring as they can be—are in principle predictable and interrogable, these ones are not. (Para.13)

 ➢ Doctors become ***inured*** to death.

13. **interrogable** /ɪnˈtɛrəgəbəl/ *adj*. That can be interrogated for information; that can respond to a query. 可被质询的

 ➢ Where the "dumb" fixed algorithms—complex, opaque and inured to real time monitoring as they can be—are in principle predictable and ***interrogable***, these ones are not. (Para.13)

 ➢ An online ***interrogable*** database is available.

重点短语

1. **gold rush**: A gold rush is a situation when a lot of people suddenly go to a place where gold has been discovered. 淘金热

 ➢ Part of the modern ***gold rush*** to develop self-driving vehicles, the SUV had been driving autonomously, with no input from its human backup driver, for 19 minutes. (Para.1)

 ➢ Although the ***gold rush*** is long over, San Francisco still boasts many appealing attractions including the Golden Gate Bridge, Fisherman's Wharf, and the Exploratorium Museum.

 ➢ The recent recession has stirred a modern day ***gold rush***.

2. **set off**: If something sets off something such as an alarm or a bomb, it makes it start working so that, for example, the alarm rings or the bomb explodes. 引爆(炸弹),触发(警报)

 This idiom was first used in business but came into more general use.

 ➢ They ***set*** the algorithms ***off*** and they learn and change and run themselves. (Para.5)

 ➢ Any escape, once it's detected, ***sets off*** the alarm.

 ➢ Someone ***set off*** a fire extinguisher.

3. **hold sway**: control; reign or rule 支配,统治

 ➢ This has revolutionized areas of medicine, science, transport, communication, making it easy to understand the utopian view of computing that ***held sway*** for many years. (Para.7)

 ➢ Bad elements ***hold sway***, while good people are pushed around. The bad eggs wielded power, while the good people were oppressed.

➢ Yet the theory continues to ***hold sway***.

4. **beyond question**: definitely, certainly 毫无疑问地,的确(SYN) without question

➢ In her 2016 book *Weapons of Math Destruction*, Cathy O'Neil, a former math prodigy who left Wall Street to teach and write and run the excellent mathbabe blog, demonstrated ***beyond question*** that, far from eradicating human biases, algorithms could magnify and entrench them. (Para. 9)

➢ To my mind, Mark Twain was ***beyond question*** the large man of his time.

➢ The military application though is ***beyond question***: twice as fast, three times the payload, five times the range of any comparable helicopter.

5. **fight tooth and nail**: If you fight tooth and nail for something, you fight as hard as you can to get it or achieve it. 奋力作战,拼命

➢ O'Neil called for "algorithmic audits" of any systems directly affecting the public, a sensible idea that the tech industry will ***fight tooth and nail***, because algorithms are what the companies sell; the last thing they will volunteer is transparency. (Para. 9)

➢ The African-Americans used to ***fight tooth and nail*** for the right to vote.

➢ If attacked themselves, they will fiercely "***fight tooth and nail***" to avoid being wounded or captured.

6. **under way**: If an activity is underway, it has already started. /If an activity gets underway, it starts. 进行中的

➢ The good news is that this battle is ***under way***. (Para. 10)

➢ An investigation is ***under way*** to find out how the disaster happened.

➢ The yearly campaign to raise funds for the Red Cross is already ***under way***.

7. **put (something) in(to) perspective**: to clarify, appraise, or assess the true value, importance, or significance of something 清楚地认识到,正确看待

➢ To ***put this into perspective***, Google's DeepMind division has been justly lauded for creating a program capable of mastering arcade games, starting with nothing more than an instruction to aim for the highest possible score. (Para. 12)

➢ To ***put that into perspective***, this is enough electricity to provide power to nearly 11,000 homes.

➢ To ***put this into perspective***, the entire database on Wikipedia is estimated to have taken just 100 million hours to complete.

8. **way off**: completely incorrect, mistaken, or misinformed 完全错误

➢ Computers are already vastly superior to us at certain specialized tasks, but the day they rival our general ability is probably some ***way off***—if it ever happens. (Para. 12)

➢ Tom is ***way off*** about Jenny if he thinks she's the type to rat us out.

➢ Exact mathematical explanations of this diversity are some ***way off***, but people are working on them.

9. **as to**: regarding or referring to; with respect to; according to 关于，根据

➢ Between the "dumb" fixed algorithms and true AI lies the problematic halfway house we've already entered with scarcely a thought and almost no debate, much less agreement *as to* aims, ethics, safety, best practice. (Para. 13)

➢ ***As to*** the matter at hand, we must act firmly and without delay.

➢ They were asked to sort the costumes ***as to*** color.

难句解析

1. An array of radar and light-emitting lidar sensors allowed onboard algorithms to calculate that, given their host vehicle's steady speed of 43 mph, the object was six seconds away—assuming it remained stationary. (Para. 1)

   Paraphrase: That SUV was equipped with advanced radar and lidar sensors, which make it possible to conduct calculation based on embedded algorithms. Since the vehicle was moving at the speed of 43 mph, the object would be hit in six seconds if it stayed static.

   解析：句子主语 an array of radar and light-emitting lidar sensors 置于句首，强调该车的配备很先进很强悍，但是结果还是撞死了人，前后形成反差，更让人反思 AI 人工智能的前景和发展。主句中用了简单的短语 allow somebody/something to do something, that 引导宾语从句。宾语从句中，有 given 的用法，表示"鉴于，由于"，相当于 because of。本句中也有破折号的用法，进一步解释说明，assuming 动名词短语作状语，其后是省略了 that 的宾语从句。

   翻译：车载雷达和激光雷达感应器迅速做出反应，车载系统算法算出，在本车以匀速 43 英里每小时的速度行驶情况下，假定前方目标静止不动，6 秒后就会撞到。

2. And how used to such incidents would we, should we, be prepared to get? (Para. 2)

   Paraphrase: And we would, should never be fully ready for such accidents!

   解析：本句是一个反问句，正常语序应该是"And how would we, should we, be prepared to get used to such incidents?", be prepared to do something 时刻准备好做某事; such incidents 这样的事件（这样的交通事故/这样的人间悲剧）。语序调整，将 such incidents 前提也是一种强调的表现，表达了一种难以置信或满腔愤怒等。

   翻译：我们会怎样、我们该怎样对这样的事件有足够的心理准备？

3. If these words sound shocking, they should, not least because Ellen Ullman, in addition to having been a distinguished professional programmer since the 1970s, is one of the few people to write revealingly about the process of coding. (Para. 4)

   Paraphrase: If these words sound shocking, they should sound shocking, not only because Ellen Ullman has been an extraordinary expert in programming since the 1970s, but also because she is one of the few people who write books to reveal the process of coding.

解析：本句中间有四个逗号，要注意划分句子结构。they should 是一个省略句，强调这些话语的确振聋发聩。because 引导原因状语从句，从句中两个逗号，in addition to ... 是插入语，除了她还是声名远扬的专业程序员，进一步解释说明她在业界举足轻重的地位和话语权。

翻译：如果这些话听起来有些令人不可思议，是因为这些话的确振聋发聩。作为专业程序员，埃伦·乌尔曼教授早在 20 世纪 70 年代就已是声名远播的专业程序员，不仅如此，她也是为数不多揭秘编码过程的作家之一。（言外之意，她说的话就是业界的标杆和圣经。）

4. In her 2016 book *Weapons of Math Destruction*, Cathy O'Neil, a former math prodigy who left Wall Street to teach and write and run the excellent mathbabe blog, demonstrated beyond question that, far from eradicating human biases, algorithms could magnify and entrench them. (Para. 9)

Paraphrase: Cathy O'Neil was a former math genius who left the financial market business in Wall Street to become a teacher and the blogger of mathbabe, and she showed without question in her book *Weapons of Math Destruction* published in 2016 that algorithms could make human prejudices worse.

解析：本句中也有四个逗号，仍要注意句子结构划分。首先要明确的是句子的主语是 Cathy O'Neil 这个人，其后的两个逗号中间的成分还是插入语，是此人的同位语，解释说明此人的背景信息，中间还有 who 引导的定语从句，介绍其年少时的非凡，其后的经历，不禁会让人肃然起敬。再看句首的短语，她 2016 年出版发行的书名，也是很有意思，令人印象深刻，会让人想到"weapons of mass destruction（大规模杀伤性武器）"。此处 mass 被换成了 math，发音相似，这一换，充分体现了作者对数学这一大规模杀伤性武器的认识，数学在她看来就好比核弹一样能量巨大。主句中 that 引导宾语从句，从句中用了三个动词，都是科技文中的正式表达，eradicate/magnify/entrench 这样大词的使用，要注意同义词的积累在论文写作中尤为重要。

翻译：凯茜·奥尼尔是一名数学神童，她曾经在华尔街工作，现在在教书、写作并管理着一个关于数学基础教育的博客 mathbabe。在 2016 年出版的《数学杀伤武器》一书中，她毫无疑问地证明了，算法远远不会消除人类偏见，相反，它将放大并巩固这些偏见。

5. Some of us dream of a citizen army to do this work, similar to the network of amateur astronomers who support professionals in that field. (Para. 11)

Paraphrase: Some of us would prefer a large crowd of ordinary people to do this work, just like in astronomy: amateurs will assist professional astronomers to finish the work that need to be done.

解析：本句运用了类比的手法，similar to the network of something 类比的写作方法可以把本来抽象的难以理解的变得很直观、易于理解。dream of somebody to do something 梦想着某人做某事。who 引导定语从句。

翻译：我们很多人梦想着有一平民大军（非专业码农）来做这项工作，就像在天文学界很多业余爱好者支持帮助天文学家完成一些任务那样。

6. Where the "dumb" fixed algorithms—complex, opaque and inured to real time monitoring as they can be—are in principle predictable and interrogable, these ones are not. After a time in the wild, we no longer know what they are: they have the potential to become erratic. (Para. 13)

Paraphrase: The "dumb" fixed algorithms are complex, incomprehensible and easy to be monitored in real time. Although those dumb algorithms are basically under control, these algorithms are beyond our control and unpredictable. After some time, we cannot recognize these algorithms any more: they have the possibility to become changeable.

解析：第一句中 where 的用法类似 while 或 whereas，表示"尽管、虽然"，引导让步状语从句。这句话的主句 these ones are not 是个省略句，省略了前面的两个形容词。且有两个破折号的用法值得注意，类似于两个小括号或者两个逗号，进一步解释说明，但是插入语中还有个并列成分也用了逗号，再用逗号就会难以分辨句子结构。第二句中 in the wild 呼应了第四段中 there's not much she doesn't know about software in the wild，此外，本句中冒号的用法，表示进一步解释说明将会出现的状况。

翻译：从理论上讲，那些"笨拙"的固定算法（复杂、不透明且易于实时监控）是可预测且可查询的，而这些算法则不是这样的。经过一段时间"自我摸索学习"后，我们已经不认识这些算法了：它们有可能会变得面目全非了。

写作技巧

Definition

Overview

The purpose of a definition essay may seem self-explanatory: the purpose of the definition essay is to simply define something. But defining terms in writing is often more complicated than just consulting a dictionary. In fact, the way we define terms can have far-reaching consequences for individuals as well as collective groups.

The definition essay opens with a general discussion of the term to be defined. You then state as your thesis your definition of the term.

The rest of the essay should explain the rationale for your definition. Remember that a dictionary's definition is limiting, and you should not rely strictly on the dictionary entry. Instead, consider the context in which you are using the word. Context identifies the circumstances, conditions, or settings in which something exists or occurs. Often words take on different meanings depending on the context in which they are used. For example, the ideal leader in a battlefield setting could likely be very different than a leader in an elementary school setting. If a context is missing from the essay, the essay may be too short or the main points could be confusing or misunderstood.

The remainder of the essay should explain different aspects of the term's definition.

For example, if you were defining a good leader in an elementary classroom setting, you might define such a leader according to personality traits: patience, consistency and flexibility. Each attribute would be explained in its own paragraph.

To illustrate this, we will take one paragraph for an example.

Sample Paragraph Analysis

➢ **Sample Paragraph**

(S1) Few subjects are more constantly or fervidly discussed right now than algorithms. (S2) But what is an algorithm? (S3) In fact, the usage has changed in interesting ways since the rise of the internet—and search engines in particular—in the mid-1990s. (S4) At root, an algorithm is a small, simple thing; a rule used to automate the treatment of a piece of data. (S5) If a happens, then do b; if not, then do c. (S6) This is the "if/then/else" logic of classical computing. If a user claims to be 18, allow them into the website; if not, print "Sorry, you must be 18 to enter". (S7) At core, computer programs are bundles of such algorithms, recipes for treating data. (S8) On the micro level, nothing could be simpler. (S9) If computers appear to be performing magic, it's because they are fast, not intelligent.

➢ **Analysis**

This paragraph first highlights the popularity of algorithms (S1). Then, the author asks a question, "What is an algorithm?" which triggers readers to think (S2). Its definition is not given immediately. Rather, the author gives us a hint about the context of how to define algorithm in a dynamic way, but not from a static point of view (S3). Then he goes back to explain the basics and logic of algorithm, as shown in Sentences 4 – 5. To make it reader-friendly, the author applies the logic to a case of entry problem. Then, the author points out the real essence of computer programs and builds a connection between algorithm and these programs, providing readers a fresh perspective (S7 & S8). Sentence 9 reveals the fact that computers are repeating certain algorithms, justifying his statement in Sentence 7. Moreover, the following paragraphs continue to explain the various facets of it, so that we can know more about the "algorithm" in reality.

Get started on your own

Directions: Read Paragraph 12 carefully and write an analysis paragraph by identifying definition.

篇章分析

This article starts with a car accident which draws our enormous attention to self-driving vehicles, and its supporting technologies—artificial intelligence (AI). The death of a woman hit by a self-driving car highlights an unfolding technological crisis, as code piled on code creates "a universe no one fully understands". Then the author talks about "What is an algorithm?" In this part, the article illustrates the historical change of the algorithm's meanings, from a simple rule to recipes for treating data, to any large, complex decision-making software system, or any means of taking an array of input of data and assessing it quickly, to independent entities with lives of their own, to algorithms doing what they've been programmed to do, to human-like artificial general intelligence, or AGI. Finally, this article presents the problem, that is, once an algorithm is learning, we no longer know to any degree of certainty what its rules and parameters are. The algorithms probably become unstable and unpredictable.

We visualize the text structure by means of a mind map.

Franken-Algorithms: The Deadly Consequences of Unpredictable Code

- **Introduction (Paras. 1 – 5)**
  - The car accident (Paras. 1 – 2)
  - Ellen Ullman's comments on this incident(Paras. 3 – 5)
- **What is an algorithm? (Paras. 6 – 13)**
  - The beginning and development of algorithm (Paras. 6 – 8)
  - Algorithmic revolution (Paras. 9 – 10)
  - "Dumb" algorithms (Paras. 11 – 12)
  - Problematic halfway house (Para. 13)

课堂提问

- According to the text, "was this algorithmic tragedy inevitable?" What should we do to avoid this kind of incident from happening? (Para. 2)
- According to the text, why shouldn't we consider this type of algorithm so meekly? (Para. 9)
- Why can we call these algorithms "dumb"? (Para. 12)
- What is the problem presented at the end of the text? How should we deal with it? (Para. 13)

教学建议

Find out the original article of this text, especially the final part of the article, so that we can know the author's opinion about the future solution to the problem presented at the end of the text. The students are well advised to conduct an intensive reading of the latter part, to gain a better understanding of regulating AI technology.

B. 课堂讨论模块

学习时间

2 hours

讨论内容

- Let students present the various applications of AI and their future.
- Exemplify the applications of AI in our everyday life.

教学方法

heuristic teaching; group discussion; class presentation

组织形式

- To divide students into several groups and choose a student from each group to show his or her PPT on the applications of AI and their future.
- To allow students to ask any question concerning the content of the text.

参考问题

- What is an algorithm?
- What does true AI mean for you?
- Besides self-driving cars, what other applications of AI do you know?

课后练习

Refer to the exercises in Unit Five of the textbook.

练习答案

Part 1 Reading Comprehension

1. Directions: The reading passage has 13 paragraphs. Which paragraph contains the following information? Write the correct number, 1 - 13, in blanks 1)- 5).

1) Para.6 2) Para.8 3) Para.9 4) Para.12 5) Para.13

2. Directions: Paraphrase the following sentences.

1) Because the computer is not allowed to evade, it gave control back to the human driver, but he wasn't paying attention.

2) Algorithms are more constantly and hotly discussed than any other subjects.

3) A more portentous and ambiguous meaning emerge in recent years./Recent years have witnessed the emergence of a more portentous and ambiguous meaning.

4) Bias can cause harm even without an ill intent.

5) The opposite side is the human-like artificial general intelligence that may be impossible.

Part 2 Words and Expressions

3. Directions: Choose proper words from the following word bank, and fill in blanks in their right forms.

1) dreadful 2) revealing 3) intervened 4) rivaling 5) magnified
6) barred 7) emerged 8) eradicate 9) fit 10) allowing

Part 3 Translation

4. Directions: Translate the following sentences from the reading passage into Chinese.

1）起初，该计算机一无所获；几秒钟后，它发现自己刚才是在处理另一辆车，并期盼着那辆车能够开走，这样就可以不对其采取其他特别行动。

2）这彻底改变了医学、科学、交通、通信等领域，使得多年来占据主流的计算机乌托邦观念更加深入人心。

3）Facebook和Google这样的公司已经出售并保护了自己的算法，这是建立在承认算法之客观性的基础上的，这种客观性要求算法能够利用数学式的客观且不带模糊情绪，对一组条件进行衡量。

4）凯茜·奥尼尔是一名数学神童，她曾经在华尔街工作，现在在教书、写作并管理着一个关于数学基础教育的博客“mathbabe”。在2016年出版的《数学杀伤武器》一书中，她毫无疑问地证明了，算法远远不会消除人类偏见，相反，它将放大并巩固这些偏见。

5）在某些专业任务上，计算机已经远远优于我们了，但距离全面性赶超可能还很遥远。

Part 4 Sentence Structure

5. **Directions**: Combine the following sentences in each group into a complex sentence.

1) The overall result has been to make entrance to professional geological journals harder for amateurs, a result that has been reinforced by the widespread introduction of refereeing, first by national journals in the 19th century and then by several local geological journals in the 20th century.

2) While in America the trend started as a reaction to the economic decline—after the mass redundancies caused by downsizing in the late 1980s—and is still linked to the politics of thrift, in Britain, at least among the middle-class down shifters of my acquaintance, we have different reasons for seeking to simplify our lives.

3) Nancy Dubler, director of Montefiore Medical Center, contends that the principle will shield doctors who strongly insisted that they could not give patients sufficient mediation to control their pain if that might hasten death.

4) Built out of a wooden tool shed, the small writing room in which Virginia Woolf penned many of her famous novels stood in the garden of a house she bought with her husband in 1919.

5) The Aswan Dam, which stopped the Nile flooding but deprived Egypt of the fertile silt that floods left, now barely generates electricity.

Part 5 Academic Writing Skills

6. **Directions**: Read the following sentences and try to make them briefer and more concise.

1) Much research has been done on position estimation in ad hoc networks.

2) Note, however, that generally the uncertainty of the estimated translation parameters is considerably larger than the actual magnitude of their values.

3) One advantage of the method is that even a small subset of the coefficients of the carrier can reconstruct the DEM and texture.

4) The lengths (norm) of these columns are equal.

5) Assistance begun in 2007 led to a method that produced long-term improvement.
6) To analyze the resolution of the hypothesis, transformation of the data is necessary.
7) We found that the proposed algorithm performs better especially when the computation time is relatively small.
8) It has been eliminated because that they are likely to contribute to the separation between classes.

Unit Six
Bitcoin

Section A The Future of Cryptocurrencies: Bitcoin and Beyond

文章主旨

This text tells us the history of Bitcoin, and the related blockchain technology, which includes an overview, a detailed description of its working mechanism, and the future development.

教学目标

- To gain a clear understanding of the history of Bitcoin.
- To master the technical words and expressions related to Bitcoin.
- To be able to use the knowledge learned to discuss issues about Bitcoin.

学习时间

4 hours (2 hours for the text; 2 hours for discussion)

A. 课堂讲授模块

预习要求

- To learn and recite the new words.
- To grasp the main idea of the text after reading.
- To search for materials related to Bitcoin.

学习时间

2 hours

教学方法

heuristic teaching; project-based teaching; task-driven teaching; group discussion;

self-study and peer learning

组织形式

- Let the students work in groups to discuss the text structure and its main idea based on fast reading, and to draw a simple mind-map as well.
- Summarize key technical terms, words and phrases, and sentence patterns in articles involving such technologies as block chain, bitcoin, etc.
- Let the students discuss in groups the learning gains based on their fields of research, and a presentation is expected.
- Analyze the complex sentences and technical issues. Spare some time to respond to any questions from the students.

背景知识

1. Blockchain

A blockchain (区块链) is a growing list of records, called blocks, which are linked using cryptography. Each block contains a cryptographic hash of the previous block, a timestamp, and transaction data (generally represented as a merkle tree root hash). By design, a blockchain is resistant to modification of the data. It is "an open, distributed ledger that can record transactions between two parties efficiently and in a verifiable and permanent way". For use as a distributed ledger, a blockchain is typically managed by a peer-to-peer network collectively adhering to a protocol for inter-node communication and validating new blocks. Once recorded, the data in any given block cannot be altered retroactively without alteration of all subsequent blocks, which requires consensus of the network majority. Although blockchain records are not unalterable, blockchains may be considered secure by design and exemplify a distributed computing system with high Byzantine fault tolerance. Decentralized consensus has therefore been claimed with a blockchain.

2. WikiLeaks

WikiLeaks (维基解密) is an international non-profit organization that publishes secret information, news leaks, and classified media provided by anonymous sources. Its website, initiated in 2006 in Iceland by the organization Sunshine Press, claims a database of 10 million documents in 10 years since its launch.

3. GHash. IO

GHash. IO (全球知名比特币矿池), founded in 2013, is a bitcoin mining pool which allows bitcoins to be mined using personal hardware or cloud-based mining power. The collective value of the bitcoin mined in this pool was over $200 million in its first year. GHash. IO works in conjunction with the CEX. IO bitcoin exchange. Apart from mining bitcoin, GHash. IO hosts a Multipool for mining altcoins, as well as separate pools for mining Litecoin, Dogecoin, Auroracoin and Darkcoin. Altcoin mining options are available for independent miners, while bitcoin mining can also be done in the cloud by purchasing cloud-based mining power on CEX. IO Exchange.

CEX. IO is a Bitcoin exchange and cloud mining provider possessing Ghash. io pool, established in London, 2013. As an online digital currency exchanger, CEX. IO offers trading Bitcoins for fiat money, such as USD, EUR and RUB. The exchange charges 0. 2% commission on each trade operation.

4. Ethereum

Ethereum is a public blockchain platform with programmable transaction functionality. It provides a decentralized virtual machine that can execute peer-to-peer contracts using a crypto asset called Ether (unofficial code ETH).

Ethereum was initially proposed by Vitalik Buterin in late 2013 and in 2014 he described it as "A Next-Generation Cryptocurrency and Decentralized Application Platform". Development was funded by a crowd sale in August 2014, and the genesis block, marking the initial pre-beta live release of the Ethereum project, occurred on 30 July 2015. The Ethereum software project was initially developed by a Swiss company, Ethereum Switzerland GmbH (EthSuisse) and a Swiss non-profit foundation, the Ethereum Foundation.

5. Vitalik Buterin

Vitalik Buterin is a programmer & writer. He is primarily known as a co-founder of Ethereum, and as a co-founder of *Bitcoin Magazine*. In 2014, Buterin won the World Technology Award for the co-creation and invention of Ethereum.

6. Encryption

In cryptography, encryption is the process of encoding messages or information in such a way that only authorized parties can read it. Encryption does not of itself prevent interception, but denies the message content to the interceptor. In an encryption scheme, the intended communication information or message, referred to as plaintext, is encrypted using an encryption algorithm, generating ciphertext that can only be read if decrypted. For technical reasons, an encryption scheme usually uses a pseudo-random encryption key generated by an algorithm. It is in principle possible to decrypt the message without possessing the key, but, for a well-designed encryption scheme, large computational resources and skill are required. An authorized recipient can easily decrypt the message with the key provided by the originator to recipients, but not to unauthorized interceptors.

7. JP Morgan Chase

JP Morgan Chase & Co. is an American multinational banking and financial services holding company headquartered in New York City. It is the largest bank in the United States, and the world's sixth largest bank by total assets, with total assets of $2. 35 trillion. Moreover, it is the sixth largest public company in the world according to the

Forbes Global 2000. It is a major provider of financial services, and according to Forbes magazine is the world's sixth largest public company based on a composite ranking. The hedge fund unit of JPMorgan Chase is the second largest hedge fund in the United States. The company was formed in 2000, when Chase Manhattan Corporation merged with J. P. Morgan & Co.

JP Morgan Chase is one of the Big Four banks of the United States, along with Bank of America, Citigroup, and Wells Fargo. According to Bloomberg, as of October 2011, JPMorgan Chase had surpassed Bank of America as the largest U.S. bank by assets.

8. Initiative for Cryptocurrencies and Contracts (IC3)

IC3（加密货币及合约计划）is an initiative of faculty members at Carnegie Mellon University, Cornell University, Cornell Tech, EPFL, ETH Zurich, UC Berkeley, University College London, UIUC and the Technion. It's based at the Jacobs Technion-Cornell Institute at Cornell Tech in NYC.

Cryptocurrencies and smart contracts are emerging into a rich spectrum of new financial instruments and business tools, and blending finance with computer science in unprecedented ways. IC3 is collaborating with domain experts in finance and banking, entrepreneurs, regulators, and open source software communities to move these blockchain-based solutions from today's white boards and proof-of-concepts to tomorrow's fast and reliable financial systems of execution and record.

See more on www.initc3.org.

9. Game Theory

Game theory is "the study of mathematical models of conflict and cooperation between intelligent rational decision-makers". Game theory is mainly used in economics, political science, and psychology, as well as logic, computer science, biology and poker. Originally, it addressed zero-sum games, in which one person's gains result in losses for the other participants. Today, game theory applies to a wide range of behavioral relations, and is now an umbrella term for the science of logical decision making in humans, animals, and computers.

Game theory has been widely recognized as an important tool in many fields. With the Nobel Memorial Prize in Economic Sciences going to game theorist Jean Tirole in 2014, eleven game-theorists have now won the economics Nobel Prize. John Maynard Smith was awarded the Crafoord Prize for his application of game theory to biology.

10. Silk Road

Silk Road was an online black market and the first modern darknet market, best known as a platform for selling illegal drugs. As part of the dark web, it was operated as a Tor hidden service, such that online users were able to browse it anonymously and securely without potential traffic monitoring. The website was launched in February 2011; development had begun six months prior. Initially there were a limited number of new seller accounts available; new sellers had to purchase an account in an auction. Later, a fixed fee was charged for each new seller account.

In October 2013, the Federal Bureau of Investigation (FBI) shut down the website and arrested Ross William Ulbricht under charges of being the site's pseudonymous founder "Dread Pirate Roberts". On 6 November 2013, Silk Road 2.0 came online, run by former administrators of Silk Road. It too was shut down and the alleged operator was arrested on 6 November 2014 as part of the so-called "Operation Onymous".

Ulbricht was convicted of seven charges related to Silk Road in U.S. Federal Court in Manhattan and was sentenced to life in prison without possibility of parole. Further charges alleging murder-for-hire remain pending in Maryland.

11. Ripple Labs

The company Ripple is the creator and a developer of the Ripple payment protocol and exchange network. Originally named Opencoin and renamed Ripple Labs until 2015, the company was founded in 2012 and is based in San Francisco, California.

12. Spotify

Spotify (声破天——流媒体音乐平台) is a Swedish commercial music streaming, podcast, and video service that provides digital rights management-protected content from record labels and media companies. It is available in most of the Americas, Western Europe, and Oceania. Music can be browsed or searched by artist, album, genre, playlist, or record label.

Spotify operates under a freemium business model, with two music streaming tiers: Spotify Free and Spotify Premium. Benefits of the Premium subscription include the removal of advertisements, improved audio quality, and the user can download music to their device for offline listening.

13. Trial and Error

Trial and error (试错法) is a fundamental method of solving problems. It is characterized by repeated, varied attempts which are continued until success, or until the agent stops trying.

Trial and error is also a heuristic method of problem solving, repair, tuning, or obtaining knowledge. In the field of computer science, the method is called generate and test. In elementary algebra, when solving equations, it is "guess and check".

This approach can be seen as one of the two basic approaches to problem solving, contrasted with an approach using insight and theory. However, there are intermediate methods which for example, use theory to guide the method, an approach known as guided empiricism.

重点词汇

1. **cryptography** /krɪpˈtɒgrəfɪ/ (also cryptology) *n*. the science or study of analysing and

deciphering codes, ciphers, etc. 密码学

➢ When the digital currency Bitcoin came to life in January 2009, it was noticed by almost no one apart from the handful of programmers who followed ***cryptography*** discussion groups. (Para. 1)

➢ Even if the data is not sensitive or personal, it should be secured with ***cryptography*** when transported to and from, and manipulated in, the cloud.

2. **quixotic** /kwɪkˈsɒtɪk/ *adj*. If you describe someone's ideas or plans as quixotic, you mean that they are imaginative or hopeful but unrealistic. 不切实际的[正式]

➢ And its purpose seemed ***quixotic***: Bitcoin was to be a "cryptocurrency", in which strong encryption algorithms were exploited in a new way to secure transactions. (Para. 1)

➢ He has always lived his life by a hopelessly ***quixotic*** code of honour.

3. **cryptocurrency** /ˈkrɪptəʊkʌrənsi/ *n*. A cryptocurrency (or crypto currency) is a medium of exchange using cryptography to secure the transactions and to control the creation of new units. 加密货币

➢ And its purpose seemed quixotic: Bitcoin was to be a "***cryptocurrency***", in which strong encryption algorithms were exploited in a new way to secure transactions. (Para. 1)

➢ It is safer to participate with the ***cryptocurrency*** as any payment is easy to check and track.

4. **pseudonym** /ˈsjuːdənɪm/ (pseudonyms) *n*. A pseudonym is a name that someone, usually a writer, uses instead of his or her real name. 假名，笔名

➢ Users' identities would be shielded by ***pseudonyms***. (Para. 1)

➢ Even his name is a ***pseudonym***, all in an effort to protect his family, friends and contacts.

5. **anonymity** /ænəˈnɪmətɪ/ *n*. the state of being anonymous, nameless 匿名

➢ Some of this growth is attributable to criminals taking advantage of the ***anonymity*** for drug trafficking and worse. (Para. 2)

➢ For superheroes, it serves as their symbol in fighting evil and sometimes provides them with the ***anonymity*** they need to protect their private lives and families.

6. **streamline** /ˈstriːmlaɪn/ *v*. To streamline an organization or process means to make it more efficient by removing unnecessary parts of it. 提高……效率

➢ But the system is also drawing interest from financial institutions such as JP Morgan Chase, which think it could ***streamline*** their internal payment processing and cut international transaction costs. (Para. 2)

➢ To ***streamline*** time drafting documents, create a forms bank for documents you frequently create and for those you may need to draft in the future.

7. **entrepreneur** /ˌɒntrəprəˈnɜː(r)/ *n*. An entrepreneur is a person who sets up businesses

and business deals. 创业者[商业]

➢ What fascinates academics and ***entrepreneurs*** alike is the innovation at Bitcoin's core. (Para. 3)

➢ To be an ***entrepreneur***, you need to be an independent, outgoing risk taker as you establish your own business or company.

8. **ledger** /ˈledʒə(r)/ *n*. A ledger is a book in which a company or organization writes down the amounts of money it spends and receives. 分类账[商业]

➢ Known as the block chain, it serves as the official online ***ledger*** of every Bitcoin transaction, dating back to the beginning. (Para. 3)

➢ The ***ledgers*** and account books had all been destroyed.

9. **gyrate** /dʒaɪˈreɪt/ *v*. If you gyrate, you dance or move your body quickly with circular movements. 旋转

➢ One result is that the market price has ***gyrated*** spectacularly—especially in 2013, when the asking price soared from $13 per bitcoin in January to around $1,200 in December. (Para. 14)

➢ As the global economy continues to ***gyrate***, you'll hear more and more people calling for the Federal Reserve to either lower or raise interest rates.

10. **profligate** /ˈprɒflɪgət/ *adj*. 1) shamelessly immoral or debauched 放荡的,行为不检点的; 2) wildly extravagant or wasteful 挥霍的,浪费的; *n*. 3) a profligate person 放荡的人,浪子,肆意挥霍者

➢ Another problem is the ***profligate*** amount of electricity used in Bitcoin mining. (Para. 19)

➢ Their ***profligate*** lifestyle resulted in bankruptcy.

重点短语

1. **be attributable to**: to regard as arising from a particular cause or source 是因为,是由于

➢ Some of this growth ***is attributable to*** criminals taking advantage of the anonymity for drug trafficking and worse. (Para. 2)

➢ In fact, personality resemblances between biological relatives ***are attributable*** almost entirely ***to*** heredity, rather than environment.

➢ To determine whether differences in national trends in tuberculosis incidence ***are attributable to*** the variable success of control programmes or to biological, social and economic factors.

2. **date back to**: to have origins that extend back to the time of someone or something 追溯到

➢ Known as the block chain, it serves as the official online ledger of every Bitcoin transaction, ***dating back to*** the beginning. (Para. 3)

➢ *Written records show that acupuncture **dates back to** the Song Dynasty.*

- ➢ The new technology is based on experiments that ***date back to*** at least the 1920s.

3. **shoot oneself in the foot**: to damage or impede one's own plans, progress, or actions through foolish actions or words 搬起石头砸自己的脚,自讨苦吃
   - ➢ ... the Bitcoin block chain could be "the most important invention of the 21st century"—if only Bitcoin were not constantly ***shooting itself in the foot***. (Para. 5)
   - ➢ He'd have a real shot at winning the election if he didn't keep ***shooting himself in the foot*** with such inflammatory remarks.
   - ➢ I think we ***shot ourselves in the foot*** by firing her, because she knew more about the project than anyone else.
4. **thefts and seizures** 巧取豪夺

   theft: the act of stealing; unlawfully taking and carrying away the property of another: robbery, burglary, plunder

   seizure: the act of taking quick and forcible possession: confiscation, expropriation
   - ➢ ... there have been more than 40 known ***thefts and seizures*** of bitcoins, several incurring losses of more than $1 million apiece. (Para. 6)
   - ➢ Art ***theft*** is now part of organized crime.
   - ➢ "Arrest" means the detention of a ship by judicial process to secure a maritime claim, but does not include the ***seizure*** of a ship in execution or satisfaction of a judgment.
5. (**be**) **akin to**: having similar characteristics, properties, etc. 类似于
   - ➢ DigiCash went bankrupt in 1998—partly because it had a centralized organization ***akin to*** a traditional bank, yet never managed to fit in with the financial industry and its regulations. (Para. 9)
   - ➢ This problem ***is akin to*** the one we had last year.
   - ➢ It's an activity more ***akin to*** gardening than to reading.
6. **manage to fit in with**: try to become assimilated into and accepted by a group 设法适应
   - ➢ DigiCash went bankrupt in 1998—partly because it had a centralized organization akin to a traditional bank, yet never ***managed to fit in*** with the financial industry and its regulations. (Para. 9)
   - ➢ They could ***manage*** their work lives ***to fit in*** with the daily routines of school drop-off and cooking dinner.
   - ➢ Most people who come from other countries ***manage to fit in with*** the way of life here.
7. **trial and error**: a process of determining the correct way in which to do something by making multiple attempts and learning from any possible failures or mistakes 反复试验,尝试错误法
   - ➢ The winner is the first to broadcast a "proof of work"—a solution showing that he or she has solved an otherwise meaningless mathematical puzzle that involves

encrypted data from the previous block, and lots of computerized ***trial and error***. (Para. 11)

➢ Human beings were not the pinnacle of a purposeful creation; like everything else, they evolved by ***trial and error*** and God had no direct hand in their making.

➢ During the period of ***trial and error***, forerunners will encounter unexpected difficulties and pressures.

8. mount against: to instigate, prepare, or set in motion some action or movement in opposition to someone or something 攻击,损害,批评,对……产生不利影响

➢ Successful "51% attacks"—efforts to dominate mining power—have already ***been mounted against*** smaller cryptocurrencies such as Terracoin and Coiledcoin; the latter was so badly damaged that it ceased operation. (Para. 17)

➢ Reports say the Iraqi government has ***mounted*** airstrikes ***against*** the ISIS militants who seized the cities of Tikrit and Mosul.

➢ An infected nurse's arrival at a Washington-area hospital topped the news in the U.S. as criticism ***mounted against*** the president, along with accusations that his administration has not done enough to protect Americans.

9. waltz off with sth.: rob, steal, seize ... something 毫不费力地获取某物

➢ Their supposition is that miners would not trust each other enough to form into pools if their fellow pool members could easily ***waltz off with*** the rewards without sharing. (Para. 18)

➢ They just picked the thing up and ***waltzed off***. Nobody asked them any questions.

10. status quo: (from Latin) the situation as it is now, or as it was before a recent change 现状

➢ However, he adds that technologies such as music taping and the internet were also considered extralegal at first, and seemed threatening to the ***status quo***. (Para. 25)

➢ The ***status quo*** and progress in reaction wetting, interfacial reaction, joint strength and partial transient liquid-phase bonding are reviewed in this paper.

➢ The conservatives are keen to maintain the ***status quo***.

难句解析

1. It is also the data structure that allows those records to be updated with minimal risk of hacking or tampering—even though the block chain is copied across the entire network of computers running Bitcoin software, and the owners of those computers do not necessarily know or trust one another. (Para. 3)

Paraphrase: The whole network of computers running Bitcoin software, whose owners don't even need to trust or even know each other, stores a copy of a data structure named block chain. Thus, the ledger of all Bitcoin transactions could be updated at the smallest risk of hacking or tampering.

解析：全句主干是强调结构 It is ... that ..., even though 引出让步状语从句，在状语从句中又有两个并列句，由 and 引导。除了强调句型，常见到的强调形式，还有以下六类：

- 用 do\does\did＋*v*.可表强调：I do hope that you'll join the singing competition.
- *adv*.或 *adj*.可表强调(never\only\very)：I only ate a small piece of cake.
- 双重否定可表强调：They never meet without quarreling.
- what 引导的主从可表强调：What really matters is cooperation.
- 倒装可表强调(凡是倒装都可以表示强调)：Only in this way can we solve the problem.
- 比较状语从句可表强调：Nothing is more imperative than to learn from the past.

翻译：区块链副本保存在运行比特币软件的所有网络计算机上，而计算机主也不一定相互认识或信任。即便如此，正是有了这种数据结构，账本记录可以得到更新而同时黑客攻击或篡改的风险又最小化。

2. "Cryptocurrencies are unlike many other systems, in that extremely subtle mathematical bugs can have catastrophic consequences," says Ari Juels, co-director of IC3. "And I think when weaknesses surface there will be a need to appeal to the academic community where the relevant expertise resides." (Para. 7)

   Paraphrase: Ari Juels, co-director of IC3, says, "Different from many other systems, an extremely small mathematical error can lead to disastrous results for cryptocurrencies. Thus, when weak points appear, it is necessary to turn to the related academic experts for help."

   解析：直接引语中一共两个句子。第一句中 in that 的意思是"因为，既然"，引导出一个原因状语从句。第二句的主干结构是 I think 接宾语从句，而且还存在从句套从句的现象，其中 when 引导条件状语从句，而 where 引导的定语从句修饰先行词 academic community。除了 in that，还有其他一些从属连词引导原因状语从句：because, as, since, now (that), considering (that), given (that), seeing (that), for 等。举例如下：

   - DigiCash went bankrupt in 1998—partly ***because*** it had a centralized organization akin to a traditional bank. (Para. 9)
   - ***Now that*** convolutional neural networks have become the dominant approach to object recognition, it makes sense to ask whether there are any exponential inefficiencies that may lead to their demise.
   - We only show the construction of B ***since*** A can be easily obtained from the k-linear instantiation of malleable SPHF shown in Section 3.2.
   - ***Considering that*** all of these transformations have a random component, they synthesize different outputs on different machines, thus increasing the diversity of attack surfaces that are visible to attackers.

翻译：IC3 的副主任 Ari Juels 说："加密货币和其他许多系统不一样，因为极其细微的数学差错就能导致灾难性后果。我认为一旦发现系统存在缺陷，就有必要向学术界求助，从那去获取专业帮助。"

3. The winner is the first to broadcast a "proof of work"—a solution showing that he or she has solved an otherwise meaningless mathematical puzzle that involves encrypted data from the previous block, and lots of computerized trial and error. (Para. 11)

Paraphrase: The first person broadcasting a "proof of work" wins the challenge. It is about solving a mathematical puzzle that is otherwise meaningless, involving encrypted data from the previous block and lots of computerized trial and error.

解析：本句的难点在于现在分词带从句。a solution 是 a "proof of work"的同位语，从现在分词 showing 开始到结束可以视为 solution 的定语，因为动作 show 和其主语 solution 在逻辑上是主动关系，因此用现在分词 showing。而 showing 的具体动作内容是 that 引导的宾语从句，而在宾语从句中又包含了由 that 引导的定语从句修饰先行词 puzzle。现在分词带从句，举例如下：

- This success, coupled with later research ***suggesting that*** memory itself is not genetically determined, led him to conclude that the act of memorizing is more of a cognitive exercise than an intuitive one.
- We begin with the investigation of wave motion in general, ***indicating how*** the various characteristics of light depend on those of the waves of which we assume it to consist.
- ***Not knowing what*** the quantitative difference is when comparing distinct scanners with the "same" scan frequency, it's very likely that a misinterpretation of system capabilities will occur.

翻译：获胜者是第一个广播"工作量证明"的人。"工作量证明"是一个方案，表明他或她已经解决了一个涉及前一区块加密数据的原本毫无意义的数学难题，并进行了大量计算机化的试错。

4. Nakamoto's design controls the supply increase by automatically adjusting the difficulty of the puzzle so that a new block is added roughly every ten minutes. (Para. 13)

Paraphrase: The puzzle's difficulty is adjusted automatically in Nakamoto's design. Thus, a new block is added about every ten minutes and the supply increase is controlled.

解析：主句是 Nakamoto's design controls the supply increase，介词 by 接动名词 adjusting 充当方式状语，表明"控制供应增长"的方式，而 so that 则引导结果状语从句。so that 既可以引导目的状语从句(常用情态动词 may, can, might 或 could 表示目的)，相当于 in order that，也可以引导结果状语从句，注意不要两者混淆。举例如下：

- He spoke at the top of his voice ***so that*** the students at the back could hear him.

他说话声音很高，为的是后面的同学能听见。（目的状语从句）

➢ He spoke at the top of his voice, ***so that*** the students at the back heard him. 他说话声音很高，结果后面的同学都听见了。（结果状语从句）

翻译：中本聪将数学难题的难度设置成可自动调节，这样大约每10分钟生成一个区块，区块供应的增长也就得到了控制。

5. To reduce the threat from mining pools, some existing cryptocurrencies, such as Litecoin, use puzzles that call more on computer memory than on processing power—a shift that tends to make it more costly to build the kind of specialized computers that the pools favour. (Para. 18)

Paraphrase: Some existing cryptocurrencies, such as Litecoin, use puzzles requiring more computer memory than processing power, so that the threat from mining pools is cut down. This change will most likely increase the cost of building specialized computers preferred by the pools.

解析：主句是some cryptocurrencies use puzzles，句子开始用不定式to reduce ...充当目的状语，puzzles后面跟了that引导的定语从句做进一步解释说明。a shift可以视作主句的同位语，由其后that引导的定语从句来说明这种转变带来的结果，在该定语从句中又嵌套有另一个that引导的定语从句修饰先行词specialized computers。从句套从句是英语长句中常见的语言现象，在科技专业文章中，这种现象非常普遍。举例如下：

➢ It is quite obvious ***that*** the organization of such a computer becomes rather complex, ***since*** one must insure ***that*** mix-up does not occur among all the various problems and ***that*** the correct information is available for the computer ***when*** it is called for, ***but*** if not, the computation will wait ***until*** it is available.

➢ The lack of privacy is ***that*** each one ***who*** is added into the network can overhear ***what*** is being said between any two others.

翻译：为减少采矿池威胁，一些现有的加密货币（例如莱特币）采用了依赖计算机存储胜过依赖处理性能的数学难题，这一转变通常会提高采矿池偏爱的专用计算机的搭建成本。

6. However, he adds that technologies such as music taping and the internet were also considered extralegal at first, and seemed threatening to the status quo. How Bitcoin, Ethereum and their successors sit legally is therefore "something that, as a culture and society, we're going to have to come together to deal with", he says. (Para. 25)

Paraphrase: Wood, though, adds that originally people also regarded technologies like music taping and the internet as extralegal and threatening to the status quo. He says that as a culture and society, we must thus work together to see how we could make Bitcoin, Ethereum and their successors legal.

解析：第一句主干是he adds，后面接that引导的宾语从句，其主要意思是technologies were also considered extralegal，such as后面举了两个实例music taping

和 internet，seem 后面接动名词 threatening 作表语。第二句中，主语由 how 引导的主语从句充当，that 引导的定语从句修饰先行词 something，而 as a culture and society 可以看作是 we 的同位语。注意 therefore 的位置，它一般置于句首，但也可以放在句中，根据表述可以灵活调整。举例如下：

- ***Therefore***, it is computationally infeasible to generate a forgery of a signature with HA-CLS.
- It is ***therefore*** a bit surprising that an auxiliary task on identifying the correctness of word order in the response does not enhance the ability of the model on the original matching tasks.
- By combining features from multiple layers, the model was able to learn features of multiple sizes, and was ***therefore*** better at classification.

翻译：他补充说，即便是音乐录制和互联网这样的技术，最初也被认为不受法律管辖，看起来威胁到了社会现状。因此，比特币、以太币及其后继者如何合法地存在，就成了我们这个社会文化整体必须得一起去面对和解决的问题。

写作技巧

How to Develop a Paragraph: Division and Classification

Overview

A paragraph generally starts with a topic sentence characterized by abstract, yet loaded words. This leaves much leeway for further development, which can be approached by a variety of techniques. Among them, division and classification is commonly used.

To achieve it, you need to do three things. First off, zoom in on one key word or phrase which carries meaning in the topic sentence. Think about anything around the word and take it down. It might be a word, a phrase or a sentence. By doing so, you are breaking the "intimidating" topic into approachable elements. This move is the so-called "division". Next, sort out these scattered elements by labelling them based on a set principle. Note that these labels should not overlap with each other in a way that might cause chaos. So far, you have finished "classification". The last step is to justify the topic sentence in the smallest way possible. Extend each label into a sentence or sentences that can serve as supporting details or evidence. In doing so, always bear stance and purpose in mind before going too far off. Contrary to big and vague words used in the topic sentence, diction here should be clear, specific and exact.

To illustrate this, we will take one paragraph for an example, putting structure and diction into perspective.

Sample Paragraph Analysis

- **Sample Paragraph**

(S1) Yet <u>the idea caught on</u>. (S2) Today, there are some 14.6 million Bitcoin units in circulation. (S3)Called bitcoins with a lowercase "b", they have a collective market value of around $3. 4 billion. (S4)Some of this growth is attributable to criminals taking advantage of the anonymity for drug trafficking and worse. (S5)But the system is also drawing interest from financial institutions such as JP Morgan Chase, which think it could streamline their internal payment processing and cut international transaction costs. (S6)It has inspired the creation of some 700 other cryptocurrencies. (S7)And on 15 September, Bitcoin officially came of age in academia with the launch of Ledger, the first journal dedicated to cryptocurrency research.

➢ **Structure Analysis**

Sentence 1

This paragraph starts with the topic sentence in five words, which can be rephrased as "Yet the idea is popular".

Sentence 2 & Sentence 3

The popularity of Bitcoin is evidenced by the following two sentences. Each supports Sentence 1 from a different angle, breaking down the vague statement into tangible terms: units and market value. This is the first time that the author adopts division and classification.

Sentence 4, Sentences 5 - 6 & Sentence 7

These three layers, four sentences are grouped together as they are inherently doing the same thing: providing evidence as to why "the idea caught on" (S1). Or, they are trying to qualify the word "growth" (S4) in three different settings: criminals (S4), financial institutions (S5 & S6) and academia (S7). Within each, application or impact of bitcoins is specified, altogether contributing to its popularity. Once again, the author employs division and classification to exemplify his statement.

We may draw a flow chart to see how this paragraph is structured.

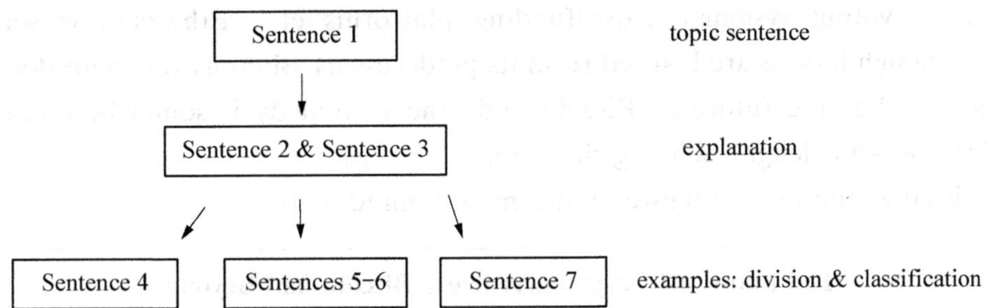

➢ **Diction Analysis**

The author creates an informative diction using numbers, synonyms and topic-specific vocabulary.

While describing the scale of Bitcoin, the author manages to show facts, using data like 14.6 million, 3.4 billion and 700. Besides, he elaborates its popularity with a chain of synonyms. Phrases such as "be attributable" "draw interest from" and "dedicated to" convey similar meaning in varied wording. Topic-specific language is ubiquitous. Scale is revealed by details like "circulation" and "market value" while application is displayed by features like "anonymity" "internal payment processing" "international transaction" "cryptocurrency research", etc.

Get started on your own

Directions: Read Paragraph 1 carefully and write an analysis paragraph by identifying division and classification.

篇章分析

This article achieves its task by addressing the best-known blockchain architecture Bitcoin first and shifting to other applications. The author introduces Bitcoin by providing informative facts including history, development and innovation with an emphasis on its template function for many other applications. Instead of continuing to extol "the most important invention of the 21st century", he takes one-step back to examine its shortcomings. Among others, security problem is the most distinctive. Far from simply identifying problems, this responsible author bends his efforts in presenting how the problems are solved. Mining is one solution, and yet it brings new pitfalls: criminal activity screening, mining competition, mining pools, overconsumption of electricity and theft. Likewise, for each mining-related problem, the author does not linger there, whining and weeping. Rather, he summons his strength in evaluating and offering the optimal fix possible until he ends up joking "We as an industry just seem to keep screwing up". So far, the author has delivered on half of his task as shown in the title "the future of cryptocurrencies: Bitcoin". He moves on to tackle the "Beyond" part by looking back to its block chain architecture and looking beyond to other applications in contracts, voting systems, crowdfunding platforms etc. Ethereum is set as an example. Though lessons are learned from its predecessor, Bitcoin, it cannot dodge legal issues equally. For the future of Bitcoin and others, remedy is somewhere out there: innovation and knowledge, echoing the title.

We visualize the text structure by means of a mind map.

The Future of Cryptocurrencies: Bitcoin and Beyond

- **Bitcoin (Paras. 1 – 22)**
  - Facts about Bitcoin (Paras. 1 – 4)
    - History (Para. 1)
    - Development (Para. 2)
    - Innovation (Para. 3)

◇ Template function (Para. 4)
○ Transition (Para. 5)
○ Problem and solution (Paras. 6 - 22)
◇ Problem: security (Para. 6)
◇ Solution: mining (Paras. 7 - 22)
◎ What is mining (Paras. 7 - 14)
◎ Problems of mining identified and solved (Paras. 15 - 22)
◇ Criminal activity screening (Para. 15)
◇ Mining competition (Para. 16)
◇ Mining pools (Paras. 17 - 18)
◇ Electricity (Para. 19)
◇ Theft (Paras. 20 - 22)
● **Beyond (Paras. 23 - 25)**
○ Introduction to Ethereum (Para. 23)
○ Problems solved: protocol audit (Para. 24)
○ New problem identified, yet unsolved: legal issues (Para. 25)
● **The future for bitcoin and beyond: innovation and knowledge (Paras. 26 - 28)**

课堂提问

- What do you know about Bitcoin?
- What are the advantages and shortcomings of Bitcoin? (Paras. 1 - 10)
- Can you describe the process of mining in your own words? (Para. 11)

教学建议

This article introduces the origin of Bitcoin, its strong and weak points, and the future development. The sentences and expressions involved are quite simple, but with lots of technical terms. Therefore, the students are well advised to conduct an extensive reading of the latter part, to gain a better understanding of prospects of Bitcoin and blockchain technology, whereas the former part should be better read intensively since it includes lots of technical terms and expression.

B. 课堂讨论模块

学习时间

2 hours

讨论内容

- To discuss the benefits and troubles that Bitcoin brings us.

➢ To use the words and expressions learned to discuss issues about Bitcoin.
➢ To use one's professional knowledge to predict the future of cryptocurrencies.

教学方法

heuristic teaching; group discussion; class presentation

组织形式

➢ Let the students as groups present a PPT about Bitcoin.
➢ Discuss their expectation of the future cryptocurrencies in groups and then present their group's idea after discussion.

参考问题

➢ Can you describe the process of mining in your own words?
➢ What are the benefits and troubles that Bitcoin brings us?
➢ What do you think is the future of Bitcoin?

课后练习

Refer to the exercises in Unit Six of the textbook.

练习答案

Part 1　Reading Comprehension

1. Directions: The reading passage has 28 paragraphs. Which paragraph contains the following information? Write the correct number, 1 - 28, in blanks 1)- 5).

1) Para. 21　2) Para. 11　3) Para. 8　4) Para. 27　5) Para. 18

2. Directions: Paraphrase the following sentences.

1) The sources of Bitcoin were not clear ... and its purpose appears unrealistic.

2) Yet the idea was very popular.

3) What allows those records to be updated with lowest risk of hacking or tampering is also the data structure.

4) ... as long as Bitcoin did not always get itself into trouble.

5) The problems related to Bitcoin quickly become obvious.

Part 2　Words and Expressions

3. Directions: Choose proper words from the following word bank, and fill in blanks in their right forms.

1) protocols　2) shielded　3) attributable　4) anonymous　5) decentralized
6) dominance　7) abuse　8) pooled　9) vulnerabilities　10) conceived

Part 3　Translation

4. Directions: Translate the following sentences from the reading passage into Chinese.

1) 数字现金高科技公司(DigiCash)在 1998 年破产——部分原因是它拥有一个类似于传统银行的中心化机构,但从未设法适应金融业及其监管法规。但 10 年后,其方方面面的哲学思想重新出现在中本聪(Nakamoto)的比特币设计方案中。

2）用户的计算机形成一个网络，其中的每台计算机都存有一个不断更新的区块链副本。

3）他的解决方案是将向账本上添加新交易的操作变成一种竞争行为：这就是现在所称的“挖矿”活动。

4）获胜者是第一个广播“工作量证明”的人。“工作量证明”是一个方案，表明他或她已经解决了一个涉及前一区块加密数据的原本毫无意义的数学难题，并进行了大量计算机化的试错。

5）无论比特币的未来如何，Narayanan 强调，比特币背后的开发者群体和学术团体都是独一无二的。“这是一个非凡的知识体系，我很确定地说 20 年内我们将在计算机科学的课堂上教授这个体系。”

Part 4 Sentence Structure

5. Directions： Combine the following sentences in each group into a complex sentence.

1）New ways of organizing the workplace—all that re-engineering and downsizing—are only one contribution to the overall productivity of an economy, which is driven by many other factors such as joint investment in equipment and machinery, new technology, and investment in education and training.

2）For the second year in a row, the Monday after Thanksgiving—so-called Cyber Monday, when online retailers offer discounts to lure holiday shoppers—was the biggest online sales day of the year, totaling some $1. 25 billion and overwhelming the sales figures racked up by brick-and-mortar stores three days before, on Black Friday, the former perennial record-holder.

3）While talking to you, your could-be employer is deciding whether your education, your experience, and other qualifications will pay him to employ you and your "wares" and abilities must be displayed in an orderly and reasonably connected manner.

4）Such large, impersonal manipulation of capital and industry greatly increased the numbers and importance of shareholders as a class, an element in national life representing irresponsible wealth detached from the land and the duties of the landowners; and almost equally detached from the responsible management of business.

5）The coming of age of the postwar baby boom and an entry of women into the male-dominated job market have limited the opportunities of teen-agers who are already questioning the heavy personal sacrifices involved in climbing Japan's rigid social ladder to good schools and jobs.

Part 5 Academic Writing Skills

6. Directions： Find as many synonyms as possible to the following italicized words and phrases in the sentences.

1）been limited to/failed to address

2）investigated/studied/analyzed/evaluated

3) found/identified/detected/observed/highlighted
4) reports/shows/details
5) modifications/alterations/adjustments
6) tests/studies
7) further evidence for/considerable insight into
8) unfounded/not well grounded/unsupported/questionable/disputable/debatable
9) potential/promising
10) in accordance with/according to/following/in line with

7. **Directions**: Read the following sentences. The first sentence is the original taken from literature, while the others (S1 - S4) are all the paraphrased versions. Analyze them to find whether they are acceptable or not in your own paper.

S1 is too identical to the original except that the author is referenced. S2 is still no essentially different from the original though several words have been changed. In S3, the sentence structure and word order have been substantially altered although the same information is intact. S4 is more serious since synonyms have been used to replace key technical words: *lung volume* different from *tidal volume*, and *breathing* different from *total ventilation*. Moreover, dropping the adjective *bilateral* alters the sense of the experimental technique. So, except for S3, all the other sentences are unacceptable.

Unit Seven
Big Data

Section A The Social Contract 2.0: Big Data and the Need to Guarantee Privacy and Civil Liberties

文章主旨

This text, by analyzing the risks that unregulated big data gathering brings about, tells us the need to establish "the social contract 2.0" to protect privacy and civil liberties.

教学目标

- To understand the benefits and the risks of big data as well as the history and content of social contract theory.
- To master the words and expressions related to big data and social contract.
- To be able to use the knowledge learned to discuss issues about big data and social contract.

学习时间

4 hours (2 hours for the text; 2 hours for discussion)

A. 课堂讲授模块

预习要求

- To learn and recite the new words.
- To grasp the main idea of the text after reading.
- To search for materials related to big data and social contract.

学习时间

2 hours

教学方法

heuristic teaching; project-based teaching; task-driven teaching; group discussion; self-study and peer learning

组织形式

- Let the students work in groups to discuss the structure and main idea of the text based on fast reading, and to draw a simple mind-map as well.
- Summarize key terms, words and phrases, and sentence patterns in the article.
- Let the students discuss in groups the learning gains based on their fields of research, and a presentation is expected.
- Analyze the complex sentences and technical issues. Spare some time to respond to any questions from the students.

背景知识

1. Social Contract

In moral and political philosophy, the social contract is a theory or model that originated during the Age of Enlightenment and usually concerns the legitimacy of the authority of the state over the individual. Social contract arguments typically posit that individuals have consented, either explicitly or tacitly, to surrender some of their freedoms and submit to the authority (of the ruler, or to the decision of a majority) in exchange for protection of their remaining rights or maintenance of the social order. The relation between natural and legal rights is often a topic of social contract theory. The term takes its name from *The Social Contract*, a 1762 book by Jean-Jacques Rousseau that discussed this concept. The heyday of the social contract was the mid-17th to early 19th centuries, when it emerged as the leading doctrine of political legitimacy.

2. Big Data

Big data is a field that treats ways to analyze, systematically extract information from, or otherwise deal with data sets that are too large or complex to be dealt with by traditional data-processing application software. Industry analyst, Doug Laney, defined Big Data in terms of the three Vs: volume, variety, and velocity. Big data often powers predictive analytics. Analysis of data sets are used to find new correlations to identify business trends, prevent diseases, combat crime and much more. Big data challenges include capturing data, data storage, data analysis, search, sharing, transfer, visualization, querying, updating, information privacy and data source.

3. Hammurabi

Hammurabi (汉谟拉比) (c. 1810 – c. 1750 BC) was the sixth king of the First Babylonian dynasty (古巴比伦第一王朝) of the Amorite (阿摩利人) tribe reigning from c. 1792 BC to c. 1750 BC. Hammurabi is best known for having issued the Code of Hammurabi (汉谟拉比法典), which he claimed to have received from Shamash, the

Babylonian god of justice. Unlike earlier Sumerian law codes, which had focused on compensating the victim of the crime, the Law of Hammurabi was one of the first law codes to place greater emphasis on the physical punishment of the perpetrator. It prescribed specific penalties for each crime and is among the first codes to establish the presumption of innocence. Although its penalties are extremely harsh by modern standards, they were intended to limit what a wronged person was permitted to do in retribution.

Hammurabi was seen by many as a god within his own lifetime. After his death, his military accomplishments became de-emphasized and his role as the ideal lawgiver became the primary aspect of his legacy. Even after the empire he built collapsed, he was still revered as a model ruler, and many kings across the Near East claimed him as an ancestor. Hammurabi was rediscovered by archaeologists in the late nineteenth century and has since become seen as an important figure in the history of law.

4. Grotius

Hugo Grotius (雨果・格劳秀斯) (1583 – 1645) was a Dutch humanist, diplomat, lawyer, theologian and jurist. Hugo Grotius was a major figure in the fields of philosophy, political theory and law during the sixteenth and seventeenth century. Along with the earlier works of Francisco de Vitoria and Alberico Gentili, he laid the foundations for international law, based on natural law in its Protestant side.

Grotius has also contributed significantly to the evolution of the notion of rights. Before him, rights were above all perceived as attached to objects; after him, they are seen as belonging to persons, as the expression of an ability to act or as a means of realizing something.

It is thought that Hugo Grotius was not the first to formulate the international society doctrine, but he was one of the first to define expressly the idea of one society of states, governed not by force or warfare but by actual laws and mutual agreement to enforce those laws.

5. Hobbes

Thomas Hobbes (托马斯・霍布斯) (1588 – 1679) was an English philosopher, considered to be one of the founders of modern political philosophy. Hobbes is best known for his 1651 book *Leviathan*, which expounded an influential formulation of social contract theory. In addition to political philosophy, Hobbes also contributed to a diverse array of other fields, including history, jurisprudence, geometry, the physics of gases, theology, ethics, and general philosophy.

6. Locke

John Locke (约翰・洛克) (1632 – 1704) was an English philosopher and physician, widely regarded as one of the most influential of Enlightenment thinkers and commonly known as the "Father of Liberalism". Considered one of the first of the British empiricists（经验主义者），following the tradition of Sir Francis Bacon（弗朗西斯·培根），he is equally important to social contract theory. His work greatly affected the development of epistemology（认识论）and political philosophy. His writings influenced Voltaire（伏尔泰）and Jean-Jacques Rousseau（让·雅克·卢梭），many Scottish Enlightenment thinkers，as well as the American revolutionaries. His contributions to classical republicanism and liberal theory are reflected in the United States Declaration of Independence.

7. Rousseau

Jean-Jacques Rousseau（让·雅克·卢梭）(1712 – 1778) was a Genevan philosopher，writer and composer. His political philosophy influenced the progress of the Enlightenment throughout Europe，as well as aspects of the French Revolution and the development of modern political，economic and educational thought. His *Discourse on Inequality* and *The Social Contract* are cornerstones in modern political and social thought.

8. PRISM

PRISM（棱镜计划）is a code name for a program under which the United States National Security Agency（NSA）collects internet communications from various U. S. internet companies. PRISM began in 2007 in the wake of the passage of the Protect America Act under the Bush Administration. The program is operated under the supervision of the U. S. Foreign Intelligence Surveillance Court（外国情报监视法庭）pursuant to the Foreign Intelligence Surveillance Act（《外国情报监视法案》）. Its existence was leaked six years later by NSA contractor Edward Snowden（爱德华·斯诺登），who warned that the extent of mass data collection was far greater than the public knew and included what he characterized as “dangerous” and “criminal” activities. The disclosures were published by *The Guardian* and *The Washington Post* on June 6，2013. Subsequent documents have demonstrated a financial arrangement between the NSA’s Special Source Operations division (SSO) and PRISM partners in the millions of dollars.

In October 2013，it was reported that the NSA monitored Merkel’s cell phone. The United States denied the report，but following the allegations，Merkel called President Obama and told him that spying on friends was “never acceptable，no matter in what situation.”

9. Metadata

Metadata（元数据）is “data that provides information about other data”. In other words，it is “data about data”. Many distinct types of metadata exist，including descriptive metadata，structural metadata，administrative metadata，reference metadata and statistical metadata.

➢ Descriptive metadata is descriptive information about a resource. It is used for discovery and identification. It includes elements such as title，abstract，author， and keywords.

- Structural metadata is metadata about containers of data and indicates how compound objects are put together, for example, how pages are ordered to form chapters. It describes the types, versions, relationships and other characteristics of digital materials.
- Administrative metadata is information to help manage a resource, like resource type, permissions, and when and how it was created.
- Reference metadata is information about the contents and quality of statistical data.
- Statistical metadata, also called process data, may describe processes that collect, process, or produce statistical data.

重点词汇

1. **empowerment** /ɪmˈpaʊəmənt/ *n*. the process of giving a person or a group of people power and status in a particular situation 权利赋予
   - Ultimately we must consider how specific technologies might either preserve or threaten human dignity, and thus what sorts of ***empowerment*** or regulation will be most appropriate. (Para. 1)
   - This government believes very strongly in the ***empowerment*** of women.
2. **monolithic** /ˌmɒnəˈlɪθɪk/ *adj*. (often disapproving) used to describe single, very large organizations that are very slow to change and not interested in individual people 单一庞大的
   - The idea of a social contract has a long history, dating back to various ancient cultures, ranging from the ancient Egyptians, Hammurabi, Greek, Roman, Chinese, Indian and the traditions of the three ***monolithic*** religions, Judaism, Christianity and Islam. (Para. 2)
   - This is a ***monolithic*** movie company.
3. **transcend** /trænˈsend/ *v*. (formal) to be or go beyond the usual limits of something 超出,超越(通常的界限)
   - What does this mean in an age of rapidly emerging technologies, Big Data, intense mobility and deepening connectivity and interdependence that ***transcend*** normal sovereign borders? (Para. 3)
   - The desire for peace ***transcended*** political differences.
4. **credo** /ˈkriːdəʊ, ˈkreɪ-/ *n*. a formal statement of the beliefs of a particular person, group, religion, etc. 信条
   - Now seems to be an appropriate time to reassess some of our long-held ***credos*** about our liberties, the functions of the sovereign and the limits of control. (Para. 3)

- American Express is emphasizing its “the customer is first” ***credo***.

5. **prowess** /ˈpraʊəs/ *n*. (formal) great skill at doing something 非凡的技能，高超的技艺，造诣
   - A radical increase in the mental and physical ***prowess*** of certain individuals via bio-technology and synthetic biology would nullify the presupposition of shared vulnerability, and with it a fundamental ground for the possibility of a social contract. (Para. 4)
   - He was complimented on his ***prowess*** as an oarsman.
6. **synthetic** /sɪnˈθetɪk/ *adj*. artificial; made by combining chemical substances rather than being produced naturally by plants or animals 人造的，人工(合成)的
   - A radical increase in the mental and physical prowess of certain individuals via bio-technology and ***synthetic*** biology would nullify the presupposition of shared vulnerability, and with it a fundamental ground for the possibility of a social contract. (Para. 4)
   - Boots made from ***synthetic*** materials can usually be washed in a machine.
7. **nullify** /ˈnʌlɪfaɪ/ *v*. (formal) to make something lose its effect or power 使无效，抵消
   - A radical increase in the mental and physical prowess of certain individuals via bio-technology and synthetic biology would ***nullify*** the presupposition of shared vulnerability, and with it a fundamental ground for the possibility of a social contract. (Para. 4)
   - An unhealthy diet will ***nullify*** the effects of training.
8. **palpable** /ˈpælpəbl/ *adj*. that is easily noticed by the mind or the senses 易于察觉的，可意识到的，明显的
   - Though the potential for technology to have such results is real and significant, other manifestations are far more advanced, and have already generated ***palpable*** effects on both intrastate and interstate relations. (Para. 4)
   - She went to the doctor for a breast exam, who confirmed the ***palpable*** mass and said she needed an ultrasound scan.
9. **insidious** /ɪnˈsɪdiəs/ *adj*. (formal, disapproving) spreading gradually or without being noticed, but causing serious harm 潜伏的，隐袭的，隐伏的
   - In this regard there are both more and less ***insidious*** risks relevant to any viable conception of a social contract. (Para. 6)
   - Tonight, we are going to tell you about one of the most ***insidious*** aspects of that threat.
10. **viable** /ˈvaɪəbl/ *adj*. that can be done; that will be successful 可实施的，切实可行的
    - In this regard there are both more and less insidious risks relevant to any ***viable*** conception of a social contract. (Para. 6)

➢ Will a hotel here be financially ***viable***?

11. thwart /θwɔːt/ *v*. to prevent somebody from doing what they want to do 阻止，阻挠

➢ As Michael Nielsen has persuasively shown, such technological monopolies have ***thwarted*** innovation and led to non-competitive conditions in particular markets. (Para. 6)

➢ She was ***thwarted*** in her attempt to take control of the party.

12. undermine /ˌʌndəˈmaɪn/ *v*. to make something, especially somebody's confidence or authority, gradually weaker or less effective 逐渐削弱

➢ Prior to questions of privacy and threats to civil liberties, there is another legitimate concern: the domination of big data gathering by large corporate interests ***undermines*** much of the positive effect to which such data could be put. (Para. 6)

➢ Our confidence in the team has been seriously ***undermined*** by their recent defeats.

13. fortify /ˈfɔːtɪfaɪ/ *v*. to encourage an attitude or feeling and make it stronger 增强

➢ At a certain threshold such inequalities leave a public quite at the mercy of the entities possessing this data, and ***fortify*** the possessor against any form of reprisal. (Para. 7)

➢ Her position was ***fortified*** by election successes and economic recovery.

14. reprisal /rɪˈpraɪzl/ *n*. a violent or aggressive act towards somebody because of something bad that they have done towards you 报复

➢ At a certain threshold such inequalities leave a public quite at the mercy of the entities possessing this data, and fortify the possessor against any form of ***reprisal***. (Para. 7)

➢ They shot ten hostages in ***reprisal*** for the assassination of their leader.

15. flout /flaʊt/ *v*. to show that you have no respect for a law, etc. by openly not obeying it 公然藐视，无视(法律等)

➢ The revelation of U.S. agencies wire-tapping German Chancellor Angela Merkel's phones has strained relations between the two countries primarily because such actions ***flout*** the conventions of a higher order social contract, in the international arena. (Para. 8)

➢ Some companies ***flout*** the laws and employ children as young as seven.

16. advent /ˈædvent/ *n*. the coming of an important event, person, invention, etc. 出现，到来

➢ With the ***advent*** of big data, it is not content which is required to predict behavior, but mostly "metadata". (Para. 9)

➢ In the last few decades, people have been facing great changes in their life because of the ***advent*** of new technologies.

17. infringement /ɪnˈfrɪndʒmənt/ *n*. an act of limiting somebody's legal rights 侵犯

➤ The nature of this and similar commentary from top agency officials conjoined with the knowledge that the widespread gathering of personal information has been ongoing for some time paints a grim portrait for civil liberties, and illustrates the potential consequences of their ***infringement***. (Para. 9)

➤ She said that terrorists attacking us are the real ***infringement*** on our freedom.

18. cede /siːd/ *v*. to give somebody control of something or give them power, a right, etc., especially unwillingly 割让,让给,转让

➤ Again, the theory of social contract informs us that individuals choose to ***cede*** some rights in exchange for their protection from the dismal life in a state of nature. (Para. 10)

➤ Cuba was ***ceded*** by Spain to the U.S. in 1898.

19. dismal /ˈdɪzməl/ *adj*. causing or showing the feeling of being sad 凄凉的,惨淡的

➤ Again, the theory of social contract informs us that individuals choose to cede some rights in exchange for their protection from the ***dismal*** life in a state of nature. (Para. 10)

➤ The future looks so ***dismal*** right now that he decides to go to big cities for more opportunities.

20. relinquish /rɪˈlɪŋkwɪʃ/ *v*. to stop having something, especially when this happens unwillingly (尤指不情愿地)放弃

➤ Rousseau's famous phrase that man must "be forced to be free" precisely argues that liberty can only exist where the citizen ***relinquishes*** his egoism and subordinates himself to the law created by the collective citizenry (of which he is a part): obeying popular sovereignty, the individual will not lapse back into a state of nature, which is implicitly a state of war. (Para. 10)

➤ She ***relinquished*** possession of the house to her sister.

21. tenable /ˈtenəbl/ *adj*. (of a theory, an opinion, etc.) easy to defend against attack or criticism 说得过去的,站得住脚的

➤ Recognizing the deep need for a ***tenable*** social contract going forward should thus influence policymakers to require accountability and transparency and to guard against violations of privacy. (Para. 12)

➤ The old idea that this work was not suitable for women was no longer ***tenable***.

22. enact /ɪˈnækt/ *v*. to pass a law 通过(法律)

➤ Constitutional amendments must be ***enacted*** without delay to protect citizens' privacy and liberties, in order to foster a more ethical, transparent, accountable, and dignified social order and consequently global order. (Para. 13)

➤ The authorities have failed so far to ***enact*** a law allowing unrestricted emigration.

23. accentuate /əkˈsentʃueɪt/ *v*. to emphasize something or make it easier to notice 着重,强调,使突出

➢ This is so primarily because of the emotional amoral egoism nature of man, which is ***accentuated*** in today's world by increased awareness, instant connectivity, empowerment by information and communications technologies, and deepening transnational and transcultural interdependence. (Para. 14)

➢ His shaven head ***accentuates*** his large round face.

重点短语

1. social fabric: the basic structure of a society that enables it to function successfully 社会结构

➢ The integrity of the ***social fabric*** at various strata relies upon—often unspoken—understandings held in common by individual members of those social strata. (Para. 1)

➢ The government's policies have destroyed the ***social fabric***.

➢ The country's ***social fabric*** is disintegrating.

2. in this regard: concerning what has just been mentioned 在这方面,在这一点上

➢ ***In this regard*** there are both more and less insidious risks relevant to any viable conception of a social contract. (Para. 6)

➢ I have nothing further to say ***in this regard***.

➢ The company's problems, ***in this regard***, are certainly not unique.

3. prior to: before something 在……之前

➢ ***Prior to*** questions of privacy and threats to civil liberties, there is another legitimate concern: the domination of big data gathering by large corporate interests undermines much of the positive effect to which such data could be put. (Para. 6)

➢ All the arrangements should be completed ***prior to*** your departure.

➢ ***Prior to*** the meeting, two expert panel meetings on the establishment of the new organization were held in Shanghai.

4. rest upon/on: to depend or rely on somebody/something 依赖于,取决于

➢ More importantly, the viability of the social contract, with its requirement of voluntary association, ***rests upon*** the guarantee to other would-be contractors that such enforcement is functional. (Para. 7)

➢ The success or failure of the film ***rests*** largely ***on*** the talents of the cast.

➢ Success in management ultimately ***rests upon*** good judgment.

5. at the mercy of: not able to stop somebody/something harming you because they have power or control over you 任……摆布,受……支配

➢ At a certain threshold such inequalities leave a public quite ***at the mercy of*** the entities possessing this data, and fortify the possessor against any form of reprisal. (Para. 7)

- After the boat's motor failed, they were ***at the mercy of*** the weather.
- I'm not going to put myself ***at the mercy*** of the bank.

6. **in question**：that is being discussed 讨论中的，考虑中的
   - Once again the willingness to cooperate is dependent upon sufficient transparency so that voluntary participants comprehend the rules and nature of the relationship ***in question***. (Para.8)
   - Where were you during the evening ***in question***?
   - On the day ***in question*** we were in Cardiff.
7. **in exchange for**：an act of giving something to somebody or doing something for somebody and receiving something in return 作为……的交换
   - Again, the theory of social contract informs us that individuals choose to cede some rights ***in exchange for*** their protection from the dismal life in a state of nature. (Para.10)
   - I've offered to paint the kitchen ***in exchange for*** a week's accommodation.
   - Wool and timber were sent to Egypt ***in exchange for*** linen or papyrus (纸莎草).
8. **(on the one hand ...) on the other (hand)...**：used to introduce different points of view, ideas, etc., especially when they are opposites (一方面……)另一方面，反过来说
   - Laws must be enacted to balance the countries "need to know" to keep societies safe ***on the one hand***, and accountable and transparent guarantee of civil liberties for all, at all times and under all circumstances, ***on the other hand***. (Para.11)
   - ***On the one hand*** they'd love to have kids, but ***on the other***, they don't want to give up their freedom.
   - I'd like to eat out, but ***on the other hand*** I should be trying to save money.
9. **guard against**：to take care to prevent something or to protect yourself from something 防止，提防
   - Recognizing the deep need for a tenable social contract going forward should thus influence policymakers to require accountability and transparency and to ***guard against*** violations of privacy. (Para.12)
   - Exercise can ***guard against*** a number of illnesses.
   - Nurses should ***guard against*** becoming too attached to their patients.

难句解析

1. The integrity of the social fabric at various strata relies upon—often unspoken—understandings held in common by individual members of those social strata. (Para. 1)

   Paraphrase：The unity of the social structure of various classes depends on the common and often unstated understandings held by the class members.

解析：本句主干为 The integrity relies upon understandings，the social fabric 是 the integrity 的后置定语，而 at various strata 又是 social fabric 的后置定语，两破折号之间的 often unspoken 则是插入语，后半句中的 held in common by individual members of those social strata 既可以看作是过去分词词组组成的后置定语，也可看作是省略了关系代词和 be 动词的定语从句，限制性定语从句常常可以与分词短语互相转换。举例如下：

➢ The girl ***who is sitting*** there is Ann's sister. ↔ The girl ***sitting*** there is Ann's sister.

➢ She bought a computer ***which was produced*** in China. ↔ She bought a computer ***produced*** in China.

➢ He used to live in the house ***which faced south***. ↔ He used to live in the house ***facing*** south.

翻译：各社会阶层的结构完整性依赖于各阶层成员所达成的共识，而这种共识往往是心照不宣的。

2. To take only one example of the ways in which technology might alter the conditions of a social contract, the capacity for individual enhancement through technological means suggests that the very basic sorts of equality early contract theorists were able to presuppose are no longer assured. (Para. 4)

Paraphrase: There are many ways in which technology may change the conditions of a social contract. To give just one example, the fact that individual ability can be improved through technology shows that the most basic sorts of equality assumed by early social contract theorists are no longer guaranteed.

解析：前半句是不定式引导的目的状语，其中又有 which 引导的定语从句，而后半句的主语较长，谓语为 suggests，其后是宾语从句。此处的 suggest 意为"表明"，而当 suggest 表示"建议"时，其引导的宾语从句往往用虚拟语气，即"suggest＋that＋主语＋should＋do"的形式，其中的 that 及 should 可以省略，同样用法的词语还包括一些命令性动词，如表示建议、请求、命令、主张等含义的动词。举例如下：

➢ At first, after describing my policy I would ***suggest*** that we make an appointment to meet to discuss whether they wanted to hire me.

➢ Most departments will ***insist*** that you take the core courses, even if you have had them at the MA level.

➢ These jobs also ***require*** that people be ready to get dirty and deal with physical risk.

翻译：科技能以多种方式改变社会契约条件，仅举一例，个人能力可借科技手段提升，这意味着早期社会契约理论家所假定的最基本的平等已经无从保障。

3. The revelation of U. S. agencies wire-tapping German Chancellor Angela Merkel's phones has strained relations between the two countries primarily because such actions flout the conventions of a higher order social contract, in the international arena. (Para. 8)

Paraphrase: It was revealed that U. S. agencies wire-tapped German Chancellor Angela Merkel's phones. This has led to tensions between the two countries primarily because such actions show no respect to the conventions of a higher order social contract, in the international arena.

解析：本句中需要注意的是of引导的同位语，of后面的动名词相当于一个同位语从句，此时的主语不仅是of之前的revelation，还包含of之后的内容，of也不再表示所属关系，而是一种同位关系，此类用法的形式为"名词＋of＋名词/动名词短语"。举例如下：

- ➢ The Museum of ***the City of New York*** embraces the past, present, and future of New York City and celebrates the city's cultural diversity.
- ➢ The machine was invented by John with ***the hope of winning*** his release from prison.
- ➢ The captain did it for ***the purpose of avoiding*** big rocks in the last second.

翻译：美国机构窃听德国总理默克尔手机的消息曝光，导致两国关系的紧张，这主要是因为此类行为藐视了国际舞台上更高的社会契约秩序惯例。

4. The nature of this and similar commentary from top agency officials conjoined with the knowledge that the widespread gathering of personal information has been ongoing for some time paints a grim portrait for civil liberties, and illustrates the potential consequences of their infringement. (Para. 9)

Paraphrase: Its nature is revelatory and disturbing; there are similar comments from top agency officials; we know that the widespread collection of personal information has been going on for some time—all these show that civil liberties are not well protected and there are potential consequences of their violations.

解析：本句的难点在于前半部分有三个较长的并列而且还包含一个同位语从句，谓语出现较晚，因此阅读起来比较困难，本句的谓语paints直到句子的后半部分才出现。在长句中，关键是要找到句子的谓语，抓住句子主干，这样才能正确理解句子的含义。在比较正式的文体中，谓语迟迟不出现的例子也十分常见。举例如下：

- ➢ This success coupled with later research showing that memory itself is not genetically determined, ***led*** Ericsson to conclude that the act of memorizing is more of a cognitive exercise than an intuitive one.
- ➢ In the early 1950's, for the first time, historians who studied preindustrial Europe (which we may define here as Europe in the period from roughly 1300 to 1800) ***began*** to investigate more of the preindustrial European population than the 2 or 3 percent who comprised the political and social elite.
- ➢ Perhaps the fact that many of these first studies considered only algae of a size that could be collected in a net (net phytoplankton), a practice that over-looked the smaller phytoplankton (nannoplankton) that we now know grazers are most

likely to feed on, ***led*** to a de-emphasis of the role of grazers in subsequent research.

翻译：它的性质、高层机构官员的类似评论再加上我们已经知道个人信息的大规模收集已经进行了有段时间——这些都描绘了一幅公民自由的灰暗图景，同时也说明了侵犯公民自由的潜在后果。

5. This may not be easily achievable, but "overseeing the overseers" in an accountable and credible way remains, nevertheless, a critical goal that must be reached if humanity is to feel secure, prosper and remain cooperative. (Para. 11)

Paraphrase: This may not be easily achievable, but it remains a critical goal that the overseers are supervised in a responsible and reliable way. The goal must be achieved if we want to feel secure, prosper and remain cooperative.

解析：本句中 but 连接了两个句子，其中 but 之后的句子较长，"overseeing the overseers"为主语（此处用到了头韵修辞手段），in an accountable and credible way 为方式状语，remains 为谓语，其后又有插入语、定语从句以及 if 引导的条件状语从句，本句需要注意的是句尾 if 从句的时态，"be to do"在这里表示的是"意图"，它也可以表示一种假设，此时需要用虚拟语气。举例如下：

- ➢ Even if you were to take a taxi now, you would not be able to arrive at your destination on time.
- ➢ Were I to have enough money, I would buy a large house.
- ➢ If I were to be a doctor, I would help those patients with all my efforts.

翻译：这可能不容易实现，然而，以一种负责任的、可靠的方式"监督监督人"仍然是一个重要的目标，如果人类想要感到安全、繁荣并且保持合作，就必须实现这个目标。

写作技巧

Loose Sentences and Periodic Sentences

Overview

From a rhetorical point of view, there are loose sentences (松散句) and periodic sentences (圆周句/掉尾句). A loose sentence "puts first things first", which means that it puts the main idea before all other information. After reading the first few words, readers know what the sentence is mainly about. A periodic sentence, however, is arranged in an opposite way. It puts the main idea at or near the end of the sentence and is not grammatically complete until the end of the sentence is reached. The difference in the two kinds of sentences can be clearly shown in the following examples.

- ➢ She finds that writing is much more interesting than she thought, although she is still unwilling to write much.
- ➢ Although she is still unwilling to write much, she finds that writing is much more interesting than she thought.

The main idea of the two sentences is the fact that she finds writing more interesting than she thought. The first sentence places the idea at the first part, which makes it a loose sentence. The second sentence, as the main idea is put at the end, is a periodic sentence. The first part of the first sentence is grammatically complete, while the first part of the second sentence is an adverbial clause.

Loose sentences and periodic sentences are also different in effectiveness. In a loose sentence, there is no suspense or climax. The sentence is easy, relaxed, natural, direct and informal. A periodic sentence, as it puts the most important information at the end, is more complex, emphatic, formal and literary. Because much information is piled up at the beginning, there is a strong sense of climax in periodic sentence, as is shown in the following examples.

➢ It is a truth universally acknowledged, that a single man in possession of a good fortune must be in want of a wife.

—*Jane Austen*

➢ The more expensive kind of antique shop where rare objects are beautifully displayed in glass cases to keep them free from dust is usually a forbidding place.

—*New Concept English 3*

When writing an article of science and technology or other serious issues, periodic sentences are always preferred. The proper place in the sentence for the main idea, which the writer desires to make most prominent is usually the end. This principle sometimes applies equally to the sentences of a paragraph, and to the paragraphs of a composition. However, it does not mean that loose sentences are forbidden. The choice of different types of sentences should depend on the idea and emotion that the author intends to express.

To better understand the two kinds of sentences, we will take two paragraphs in Section A as an example.

Sample Section Analysis

➢ **Sample Paragraphs**

(S1) Big data also has more immediate and troubling implications for justice, as recent analysis of U.S. National Security Agency policy and actions have demonstrated. (S2) The revelation of U.S. agencies wire-tapping German Chancellor Angela Merkel's phones has strained relations between the two countries primarily because such actions flout the conventions of a higher order social contract, in the international arena. (S3) Once again the willingness to cooperate is dependent upon sufficient transparency so that voluntary participants comprehend the rules and nature of the relationship in question. (S4) In the context of international relations, considerations both of individual privacy and state security will be profoundly influenced by the methods of information gathering undertaken.

(S5) Perhaps most striking in this regard is the volume of data being gathered. (S6) With the advent of big data, it is not content which is required to predict behavior, but mostly "metadata". (S7) It is for this reason that the NSA's former director, Michael Hayden's comment that "... we kill people based on metadata", is as revelatory as it is disturbing. (S8) The nature of this and similar commentary from top agency officials conjoined with the knowledge that the widespread gathering of personal information has been ongoing for some time paints a grim portrait for civil liberties, and illustrates the potential consequences of their infringement.

➤ **Sample Analysis**

There are eight sentences in the two paragraphs. According to the place of the main idea in each sentence, Sentences 1-3 are loose while the rest ones are periodic. Therefore, in the two sample paragraphs, periodic sentences outnumber loose ones. Because the article in Section A is a rather formal one, there are more periodic sentences in it. In the first sample paragraph, the author starts with a loose sentence, expressing his stance directly and clearly. Sentence 2 opens with an example to detail the adverbial clause in Sentence 1, knitting closely in meaning. Following that, Sentence 3 reveals the lesson learned from Angela Merkel's case, which is the necessity of "sufficient transparency" in the first half and moves on to the effect it will have in the second half. From Sentence 4 to Sentence 8, periodic sentences create more suspense and verify the author's arguments more powerfully as the paragraph develops step by step. Each sentence delivers a new idea near the end and the next one responds to it using cohesive devices either explicitly or implicitly. Sentence 4 puts the emphasis in the end to connect with the phrase "in this regard" in Sentence 5 while Sentence 5 highlights the topic of this paragraph using periodic sentence. Repeating "big data" in the beginning, Sentence 6 adopts the pattern "... not ... but" to underline "metadata", which responds to "this reason" in Sentence 7. It goes on with discussing the comment from the NSA's former director. Sentence 8 summarizes commentary like this and conveys the message that civil liberty is not only infringed but more importantly, takes its toll because of the infringement, reaching the climax.

Get started on your own

Directions: Read Paragraph 6 carefully; identify the periodic sentences and rewrite them into loose ones so that the difference in their effectiveness is better understood.

篇章分析

This article tells us the need to establish "the social contract 2.0" to protect privacy and civil liberties against the risks that unregulated big data gathering brings about. To achieve this goal, the author first explains the term "social contract" and the history of the theory before proceeding to the risks of the new technologies, which is the focus of the whole article. Then the author lists the three risks, which include technological threats to social cooperation, monopolistic control over big data as well as civil liberties, justice and privacy infringement. Through explaining these risks, the author informs us that the early social contract is under challenge because of unregulated Big Data acquisition, and there is a need to seek a balance between taking security measures through mass surveillance and protecting civil liberties and privacy. In the last part, the author gives some policy recommendations that he believes necessary to address these risks. He argues that laws must be enacted and amended to achieve the aforementioned balance; accountability and transparency are also required; violations of privacy should be stopped and big data gathering should be monitored and regulated. Finally, the author draws a conclusion: with the accentuated emotional amoral egoism of human beings in the modern world, security cannot be guaranteed unless equalities, justices, liberties and privacies are protected.

We visualize the text structure by means of a mind map.

The Social Contract 2.0: Big Data and the Need to Guarantee Privacy and Civil Liberties

- **Background (Para. 1)**
- **Social contract (Paras. 2 – 3)**
  - History (Para. 2)
  - Common thread (Para. 3)
- **Risks (Paras. 4 – 10)**
  - Technological threats to social cooperation (Paras. 4 – 5)
  - Monopolistic control (Paras. 6 – 7)
  - Justice and privacy infringement (Paras. 8 – 10)
- **Policy recommendations (Paras. 11 – 13)**
- **Summary (Para. 14)**

课堂提问

- What do you know about big data?
- Can you give some examples showing that we are benefiting from this technology?
- What are the risks of unregulated information gathering? (Paras. 4 – 10)

教学建议

Although there are not many technical terms in the text, the article is still difficult to understand because of the length of the sentences and the sociological concepts. An intensive reading of the whole article is well advised and students are encouraged to further explore the issues concerning the relationship between technology and social problems.

B. 课堂讨论模块

学习时间

2 hours

讨论内容

- To discuss the benefits and risks that big data brings us.
- To use the words and expressions learned to discuss issues about big data and social contract.
- To give some suggestions to protect liberty, privacy and justice so that big data can serve us better.

教学方法

heuristic teaching; group discussion; class presentation; debate

组织形式

- Let the students as groups present a PPT about big data and its effects on our society.
- If possible, organize a debate over whether big data makes our life easier.

参考问题

- Besides what has been mentioned by the author, what other risks do you know that unregulated information gathering might bring us?
- What are the consequences of liberty and privacy infringement?
- Can you give some suggestions to better develop the technology of big data while protecting our legal rights?

课后练习

Refer to the exercises in Unit Seven of the textbook.

练习答案

Part 1 Reading Comprehension

1. Directions: Do the following statements agree with the information given in the reading passage? In blanks 1)-5), choose

TRUE if the statement agrees with the information.
FALSE if the statement contradicts the information.
NOT GIVEN if there is no such information in the statement.

1) True (Para.4) 2) True (Para.6) 3) Not given (Para.11)

4) False (Para.10) 5) True (Para.12)

2. Directions: Paraphrase the following sentences.

1) It is self-evident that the intactness of the social structure at various classes depends on the common understandings by the members in those social classes.
2) Apparently, there is a possible threat that some monopolies will control such data.
3) A private enterprise who control a lot of personal information has the power to predict what will happen, which will make it have an edge in the shared system.
4) Big data produces the inequity in controlling data, and also makes this inequity worse.
5) Only if we have these protection measures employed, the probabilities of continuing and increased social cooperation can keep a reasonable choice in both fields.

Part 2 Words and Expressions

3. Directions: Choose proper words from the following word bank, and fill in blanks in their right forms.

1) restraint 2) undermining 3) preserve 4) enforced 5) accountable
6) employed 7) address 8) enhances 9) capacity 10) are empowered

Part 3 Translation

4. Directions: Translate the following sentences from the reading passage into Chinese.

1) 许多新技术引发了我们与这些技术的关系的问题,至关重要的是要从它们的社会和文化影响的角度来考虑。
2) 尽管大数据有许多优势,比如可以更好地应对流感疫情,更全面地了解世界粮食需求和分配能力,但由于大数据获取缺乏监管,也会导致严重的问题。
3) 此外,在垄断的情况下,即使是对最低限度社会契约所要求的合作的肤浅理解也会受到破坏。
4) 一旦达到某一临界值,这种不平等使公众完全听任这些数据所有者的摆布,并使这些数据所有者免遭任何形式的报复。
5) 必须制定法律以平衡各国的"知情需求",一方面确保社会安全,另一方面在任何时候、任何情况下以负责、透明的方式保障公民自由。

Part 4 Sentence Structure

5. Directions: Combine the following sentences in each group into a complex sentence.

1) Television, the most pervasive of modern technologies, marked by rapid change and progress, is moving into a new era, an era of extraordinary sophistication, which promises to reshape our life.
2) Those functions that describe how a computer software reacts to mechanical design, called application functions, are more often important to the engineer in engineering applications such as analysis, calculation, and simulation.
3) He is referring to the upsurge of internet in mobile television, a nascent industry at

the intersection of telecoms and media which offers new opportunities to device makers, content-producers and mobile-network operators.

4) The teachers who took part in the program also told me of their worries that they might be force-feeding their pupils information rather than stimulating the discussion necessary to ensure they grasped the importance of what they were being taught.

5) Nokia, which has made emerging markets a priority, continues to introduce low-cost phones designed for market where users do not have access to reliable internet.

Part 5 Academic Writing Skills

6. Directions: Use proper hedges to soften too direct or over-positive expressions.

1) The result *seems to show* that although the encryption has been applied, the information leak still exists.

2) We also notice that SMC conditions *are more likely to* develop when the solar wind velocity is low.

3) Although many authors have investigated how PhD students write papers, *we believe/as far as we know/to the best of our knowledge* this is the first attempt to systematically analyze all the written output (papers, reports, grant proposals, CVs etc.) of such students.

4) A loss of lock on all GPS signals simultaneously implies that users *may have to* wait for several minutes (even hours in certain cases) before obtaining cm-level precision.

5) Its application to the PYXIS arrays, however, is *somewhat* problematic.

Unit Eight
Quantum Computing

Section A Cryptography after the Aliens Land

文章主旨

This article touches upon facts about cryptography, challenges it will have when technology is fully developed, and possible solutions within human being's reach. The author takes an optimistic attitude towards future issues, though worries run deep.

教学目标

- To gain a clear understanding of the text.
- To master commonly used words and expressions.
- To be able to use the knowledge to discuss topic-related issues.

学习时间

4 hours (2 hours for the text; 2 hours for discussion)

A. 课堂讲授模块

预习要求

- To learn and recite new words.
- To grasp the main idea of the text after reading.
- To search for materials related to cryptography.

学习时间

2 hours

教学方法

heuristic teaching; project-based teaching; task-driven teaching; group discussion;

self-study and peer learning

组织形式

- Work in groups to discuss text structure and its main idea based on fast reading, and to draw a mind-map as well.
- Get familiar with commonly used words and phrases, and extract generic sentences.
- Analyze complex sentences and technical issues. Spare some time to respond to questions from students.
- Share in groups what students have learned and present a slideshow.

背景知识

1. The RSA Cryptosystem

RSA (Rivest-Shamir-Adleman) is one of the first public-key cryptosystems and is widely used for secure data transmission. In such a cryptosystem, the encryption key is public and it is different from the decryption key which is kept secret (private). In RSA, this asymmetry is based on the practical difficulty of the factorization of the product of two large prime numbers, the "factoring problem". The acronym RSA is made of the initial letters of the surnames of Ron Rivest, Adi Shamir, and Leonard Adleman, who first publicly described the algorithm in 1977. Clifford Cocks, an English mathematician working for the British intelligence agency Government Communications Headquarters (GCHQ), had developed an equivalent system in 1973; but this was not declassified until 1997.

2. Cryptography

Cryptography or cryptology is the practice and study of techniques for secure communication in the presence of third parties called adversaries. More generally, cryptography is about constructing and analyzing protocols that prevent third parties or the public from reading private messages; various aspects in information security such as data confidentiality, data integrity, authentication, and nonrepudiation are central to modern cryptography. Modern cryptography exists at the intersection of the disciplines of mathematics, computer science, electrical engineering, communication science, and physics. Applications of cryptography include electronic commerce, chip-based payment cards, digital currencies, computer passwords, and military communications.

3. Encryption Algorithm

Encryption algorithm, or cipher, is a mathematical function used in the encryption and decryption process—series of steps that mathematically transforms plaintext or other readable information into unintelligible ciphertext. A cryptographic algorithm works in combination with a key (a number, word, or phrase) to encrypt and decrypt data. To encrypt, the algorithm mathematically combines the information to be protected with a supplied key. The result of this combination is the encrypted data. To decrypt, the algorithm performs a calculation combining the encrypted data with a supplied key. The result of this combination is the decrypted data. If either the key or the data is modified, the algorithm produces a different result. The goal of every encryption algorithm is to make it as difficult as possible to decrypt the generated ciphertext without using the key.

4. Asymmetric Cryptography (Public Key Cryptography)

Asymmetric cryptography, also known as public key cryptography, uses public and private keys to enypt and decrypt data. The keys are simply large numbers that have been paired together but are not identical (asymmetric). One key in the pair can be shared with everyone; it is called the public key. The other key in the pair is kept secret; it is called the private key. Either of the keys can be used to encrypt a message; the opposite key from the one used to encrypt the message is used for decryption.

5. Symmetric Encryption Algorithms

Symmetric encryption algorithms can be divided into stream ciphers and block ciphers. Stream ciphers encrypt a single bit of plaintext at a time, whereas block ciphers take a number of bits (typically 64 bits in modern ciphers), and encrypt them as a single unit.

6. Grover's algorithm

Grover's algorithm is a quantum algorithm that finds with high probability the unique input to a black box function that produces a particular output value, using just O(√(N)) evaluations of the function, where N is the size of the function's domain. It was devised by Lov Grover in 1996. The analogous problem in classical computation cannot be solved in fewer than O(N) evaluations (because, in the worst case, the N-th member of the domain might be the correct member).

7. Shor's Algorithm

Shor's algorithm is a polynomial time quantum computer algorithm for integer factorization. Informally, it solves the following problem: Given an integer N, find its prime factors. It was invented in 1994 by the mathematician Peter Shor. On a quantum computer, to factor an integer N, Shor's algorithm runs in polynomial time (the time taken is polynomial in log N, the size of the integer given as input).

8. The Advanced Encryption Standard (AES)

The Advanced Encryption Standard (AES) is a symmetric-key block cipher algorithm and U.S. government standard for secure and classified data encryption and decryption. In December 2001, the National Institute of Standards (NIST) approved the AES as Federal Information Processing Standards Publication (FIPS PUB) 197, which specifies application of the Rijndael algorithm to all sensitive classified data.

9. One-time Pad

The one-time pad is a long sequence of random letters. These letters are combined with the plain text message to produce the ciphertext. To decipher the message, a person must have a copy of the one-time pad to reverse the process. A one-time pad should be used only once (hence the name) and then destroyed. This is the first and only encryption algorithm that has been proven to be unbreakable.

10. Information Theory

Information theory is the mathematical treatment of the concepts, parameters and rules governing the transmission of messages through communication systems. It was founded by Claude Shannon toward the middle of the twentieth century and has since then evolved into a vigorous branch of mathematics fostering the development of other scientific fields, such as statistics, biology, behavioral science, neuroscience, and statistical mechanics.

重点词汇

1. **nascent** /ˈneɪsnt/ *adj*. beginning to exist; not yet fully developed 初期的，早期的
   - ➢ Currently, quantum computing is too ***nascent*** for cryptographers to be sure of what is secure and what isn't. (Para. 2)
   - ➢ Younger artists, such as the ***nascent*** Impressionists, also admired him.
2. **spell** /spel/ *v*. to have something, usually something bad, as a result; to mean something, usually something bad 招致，导致
   - ➢ But even assuming aliens have developed the technology to its full potential, quantum computing doesn't ***spell*** the end of the world for cryptography. (Para. 2)
   - ➢ China's financial system remains fragile, and sudden currency volatility could lead to a banking crisis that could ***spell*** disaster for the world economy.
3. **inconceivable** /ˌɪnkənˈsiːvəbl/ *adj*. impossible to imagine or believe 难以想象的，难以置信的
   - ➢ And if some ***inconceivable*** alien technology can break all of cryptography, we still can have secrecy based on information theory-albeit with significant loss of capability. (Para. 2)
   - ➢ The scope of the suffering is ***inconceivable***.
4. **astronomically** /ˌæstrəˈnɒmɪkli/ *adv*. extremely; by a very large amount 巨大，极大地
   - ➢ Not just a little more difficult, but ***astronomically*** more difficult. (Para. 4)
   - ➢ Interest rates are ***astronomically*** high.
5. **upend** /ʌpˈend/ *v*. to turn somebody/something the wrong way up or onto one end 倒放，颠倒
   - ➢ Quantum computers promise to ***upend*** a lot of this. (Para. 8)

➢ All of this ***upended*** as people try to figure out what to do next.

6. dire /ˈdaɪə(r)/ *adj*. very serious 极其严重的，危急的

➢ For public-key cryptography, the results are more ***dire***. (Para. 9)

➢ For Arctic productivity, the consequences are likely to be ***dire***.

7. caveat /ˈkæviæt/ *n*. a warning that particular things need to be considered before something can be done 警告，说明

➢ There are a lot of ***caveats*** to those two paragraphs, the biggest of which is that quantum computers capable of doing anything like this don't currently exist, and no one knows when—or even if—we'll be able to build one. (Para. 10)

➢ Despite the ***caveat*** he still called it his most enjoyable birthday.

8. detour /ˈdiːtʊə(r)/ *n*. a longer route that you take in order to avoid a problem or to visit a place 绕行，绕道

➢ Maybe the whole idea of number theory-based encryption, which is what our modern public-key systems are, is a temporary ***detour*** based on our incomplete model of computing. (Para. 14)

➢ Some apps, or phone applications, even provide real-time alerts about traffic jams, accidents, and ***detours***.

9. underpin /ˌʌndəˈpɪn/ *v*. to support or form the basis of an argument, a claim, etc. 支撑，支持

➢ While there are several mathematical theories that ***underpin*** the one-wayness we use in cryptography, proving the validity of those theories is in fact one of the great open problems in computer science. (Para. 16)

➢ The technology that ***underpins*** digital currencies—the blockchain—is an important development.

10. muddle /ˈmʌdl/ *n*. a state in which things are untidy and not in order 混乱，杂乱

➢ Symmetric cryptography is so much nonlinear ***muddle***, so easy to make more complex, and so easy to increase key length, that this future is unimaginable. (Para. 16)

➢ After half an hour it's over. Bauer said it helped sort the ***muddle*** in her head.

11. detonate /ˈdetəneɪt/ *v*. to explode, or to make a bomb or other device explode 使爆炸，引爆

➢ Our nukes might refuse to ***detonate*** and our fighter jets might fall out of the sky, but we will still be able to communicate securely using one-time pads. (Para. 18)

➢ We never owned slaves, bill, or ***detonated*** nuclear weapons.

重点短语

1. allow for: to consider or include somebody/something when calculating something 考虑到，顾及

- It ***allows for*** very fast searching, something that would break some of the encryption algorithms we use today. (Para. 1)
- It will take about an hour to get there, ***allowing for*** traffic delays.
- All these factors must be ***allowed for***.

2. end up: to find yourself in a place or situation at the end of a process or period of time 最终,结果是

- If public-key cryptography ***ends up*** being a temporary anomaly based on our mathematical knowledge and computational ability, we'll still survive. (Para. 2)
- I ***ended up*** doing all the work myself.
- If you go on like this you'll ***end up*** in prison.

3. rely on: to need or depend on somebody/something 依赖,依靠

- At its core, cryptography ***relies on*** the mathematical quirk that some things are easier to do than to undo. (Para. 3)
- The charity ***relies*** solely ***on*** donations from the public.
- They had to ***rely*** entirely ***on*** volunteer workers.

4. speed something up: to make something move or happen faster 加快,加速

- Grover's algorithm shows that a quantum computer ***speeds up*** these attacks to effectively halve the key length. (Para. 8)
- They have ***speeded*** up production of the new car.
- The daring new technique dramatically ***speeded up*** the construction process.

5. fall to: to become the duty or responsibility of somebody 成为……的责任或义务

- After that, though, there is always the possibility that those algorithms will ***fall to*** aliens with better quantum techniques. (Para. 12)
- With his partner away, all the work now ***fell to*** him.
- It ***fell to*** me to inform her of her son's death.

6. a blow to: a sudden event that hurts or damages somebody/something, causing the people affected to be sad or disappointed 对……的打击

- That would be a huge ***blow to*** security and would break a lot of stuff we currently do, but we could adapt. (Para. 13)
- Losing his job came as a terrible ***blow to*** him.
- It was a shattering ***blow to*** her pride.

7. be vulnerable to: weak and easily hurt physically or emotionally 易受伤害

- Public-key cryptography ***is*** all number theory, and potentially ***vulnerable to*** more mathematically inclined aliens. (Para. 16)
- These offices ***are*** highly ***vulnerable to*** terrorist attack.
- Old people ***are*** particularly ***vulnerable to*** the flu.

8. other than：except 除了

➢ Unless mathematics is fundamentally different than our current understanding, that'll be secure until computers are made of something ***other than*** matter and occupy something other than space.（Para.16）

➢ I don't know any French people ***other than*** you.

➢ We're going away in June but ***other than*** that I'll be here all summer.

9. replace with：to remove somebody/something and put another person or thing in their place 替代

➢ Today, only crackpots try to build general-use systems based on one-time pads—and cryptographers laugh at them, because they ***replace*** algorithm design problems (easy) ***with*** key management and physical security problems (much, much harder). (Para.17)

➢ It is not a good idea to miss meals and ***replace*** them ***with*** snacks.

➢ What if drugs **were *replaced with*** electricity?

10. -ridden：full of a particular unpleasant thing 充斥……的

➢ In our ***alien-ridden*** science-fiction future, we might have nothing else.（Para.17）

➢ After an ***anxiety-ridden*** afternoon and evening, her stand-in finally called her at 11:00 PM.

➢ Most blacks still live in shoddy shacks or bungalows without proper sanitation in poor ***crime-ridden*** townships outside the main cities.

难句解析

1. But even assuming aliens have developed the technology to its full potential, quantum computing doesn't spell the end of the world for cryptography.（Para.2）

Paraphrase：However, even if quantum computing is highly advanced in the future, cryptography will not end up being broken.

解析：本句的构造为"条件状语从句+主句"。其中，assuming 为连词，表示"假定"，引导的是条件状语从句，逗号之后为主句。需注意的是，此处 assuming 不是现在分词，因此不受主句中主语 quantum computing 的影响。英文中还有许多单词形为分词，实为连词或介词，如 providing（连词）、provided（连词）、regarding（介词）、considering（连词或介词）、given（介词）等。举例如下：

➢ We'll buy everything you produce, providing of course the price is right.

➢ Provided that you have the money in your account, you can with draw up to ??800 a day.

➢ He has said nothing regarding your request.

➢ She's very active, considering her age.

➢ Considering he's only just started, he knows quite a lot about it.

翻译：但是，即便假设外星人已经充分开发了量子计算技术，也不意味着密码学的世界末日。

2. There are a lot of caveats to those two paragraphs, the biggest of which is that quantum computers capable of doing anything like this don't currently exist, and no one knows when—or even if—we'll be able to build one. (Para. 10)

Paraphrase: To the two paragraphs above regarding symmetric cryptography and public-key cryptography, there are a lot of warnings. Among them, the most threatening one is that quantum computers today can't do anything mentioned above. Plus, we don't know if we are able to invent a quantum computer, let alone when to have it.

解析：本句结构为"并列句 1＋并列句 2"。其中，并列句 1(There are ... exist)含有 which 引导的定语从句，指代主句中的 caveats。从句的结构为"主语＋系动词＋表语从句"。并列句 2 (and no one ... one)的结构为"主语＋谓语＋宾语从句(when/if)"。需要指出的是，并列句 1 中的定语从句，采用的结构是"介词＋关系代词"，用来说明其中的一部分，最高级等情况。举例如下：

- The two remaining plants, one of which was at the centre of the array, were left to grow unimpeded.
- A hidden galaxy may be just beyond the Milky Way, part of which is shown over California's Mount Lassen.
- The studies also ran up against many methodological challenges, the biggest of which centered on the old statistical saying, "Correlation does not equal causation".

翻译：对于上述两段文字，还有很多的限制。其中最大的问题是，目前尚不存在能够执行类似操作的量子计算机，而且没人知道我们何时甚至是否有能力发明一个。

3. I am less worried about symmetric cryptography, where Grover's algorithm is basically an upper limit on quantum improvements, than I am about public-key algorithms based on number theory, which feel more fragile. (Para. 12)

Paraphrase: I'm more worried about public-key algorithms than symmetric cryptography because the former is built on the weak number theory while the latter has the best solution now in quantum techniques, Grover's algorithm.

解析：此句用了"less ... than ..."的比较结构，表示"比……少"。两个对比的事物为 symmetric cryptography 和 public-key algorithms，作者分别用了 where ... 及 which ... 两个定语从句对其描述，说明原因。较为复杂的是，than 后省略了相同的部分 worried。这种现象英文中也有很多，举例如下：

- I know less now than I did before I asked.
- You obviously find him far less interesting than I do.

翻译：和对称加密算法(其中格罗弗的算法基本上是量子计算的最优方案)相比，我更担心公钥算法，因为这种基于数字理论的算法更脆弱。

4. While there are several mathematical theories that underpin the one-wayness we use

in cryptography, proving the validity of those theories is in fact one of the great open problems in computer science. (Para. 16)

Paraphrase: Although many mathematical theories can explain the one-wayness in cryptography, one question is yet to be solved in computer science as to how to prove that those theories are convincing.

解析：此句的结构为"让步状语从句＋主句"。其中，让步状语从句中含有 that 引导的定语从句，修饰先行词 theories，主句中的主语为动名词短语。while 除了表示"虽然"之外，还有"当……时""而……"。举例如下：

- While I am willing to help, I do not have much time available.
- We must have been burgled while we were asleep.
- While Tom's very good at science, his brother is absolutely hopeless.

翻译：虽然一些数学理论能够解释密码学中的单向性，但实际上，证明这些理论的有效性是计算机科学中的主要未解问题之一。

5. Unless mathematics is fundamentally different than our current understanding, that'll be secure until computers are made of something other than matter and occupy something other than space. (Para. 16)

Paraphrase: Cryptography will remain unbroken as long as mathematics has not challenged our current understanding and computers are still made of matter and control the whole universe.

解析：该句结构为"条件状语从句＋主句＋条件状语从句"。作者用了两个从句说明未来数学和计算机的变化，并指出只有出现这些变化，密码技术才有望被攻克。other than 的意思为"除了(except)"。

翻译：除非数学与我们目前的理解有根本的不同，否则在出现非物质计算机占领非宇宙空间之前，密码系统仍是安全的。

写作技巧

How to Construct an Argument

Overview

More often than not, you start writing with an opinion, whatever writing style you adopt. This goes on with defending your opinion using devices like reasoning and evidence. This toolkit has proved to be watertight.

An opinion is also called a claim, a stance an author holds. It is an answer to a question that may have long puzzled potential readers and hence motivates the writer to deliver. While putting it into words, you need to state in a clear and concise way and construct it at the beginning of a paragraph. You do not have to rush to pad the sentence or sentences with too many details. Rather, make it sound crisp. Slowly but surely entice readers to move along.

What comes next is reasoning, in which you explain what it takes to make such a statement as in the beginning. Keep questioning yourself with "why" "how" "so what", etc., in case discreet readers may object with doubts. To do so, you utilize resources like theories, common sense and scientific findings. String them in a logical way before reaching the goal.

Reasoning alone, you are still some way off in convincing readers to buy into your ideas. It is easy to understand reasoning as the brainchild, not the reality. Cliché has it that to see is to believe. Therefore, you have to find evidence that you can see, hear, or feel in reality. Draw from your past experiences. Refer to scientific data. Talk about what is happening. Anything relevant that you can find in a world of flesh and steel works out.

Before coming to the conclusion, look around for possible loopholes including objection, doubt, or alternatives. If any, work on them. Responding to naysayers will not hold you back, but rather bring you closer to what you are meant to reach.

In short, to voice what you believe, start with a claim, back it up with reasons, support it with evidence in the real world and complement it with warrants.

Sample Paragraph Analysis

➢ **Sample Paragraph**

(S1) Public-key encryption (used primarily for key exchange) and digital signatures are more complicated. (S2) Because they rely on hard mathematical problems like factoring, there are more potential tricks to reverse them. (S3) So you'll see key lengths of 2,048 bits for RSA, and 384 bits for algorithms based on elliptic curves. (S4) Here again, though, the costs to reverse the algorithms with these key lengths are beyond the current reach of humankind.

➢ **Structure analysis**

Sentence 1

The author claims that compared with symmetric cryptography in Paragraph 4, public-key encryption is more complex.

Sentence 2

This sentence reveals the reason of public-key encryption by tracing back to its mathematical root and based on that, predicts the consequence of reversing it.

Sentence 3

The author presents two methods of public-key encryption which are RSA and elliptic curves to show its complexity.

Sentence 4

The last sentence discusses the cost of reversing which strengthens the claim that public-key encryption is not an easy one.

We may draw a brief map to show how these sentences are connected.

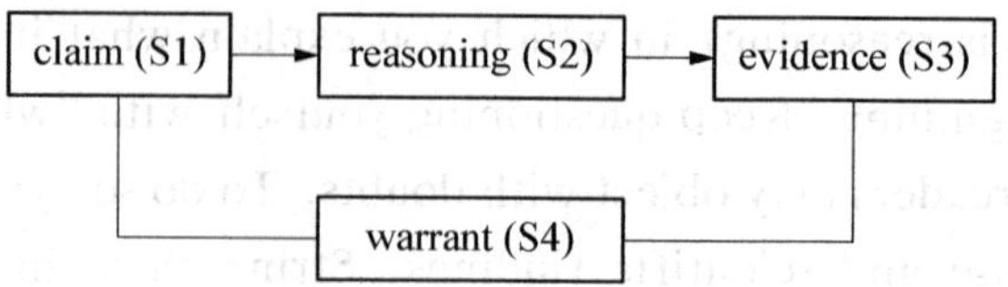

➢ **Diction Analysis**

In the topic sentence, the author makes his stance clear by using one crisp word "complicated". Following that, the word "because" shows the rationale. To support this, two examples of public-key encryption are presented: RSA and elliptic curves. Numbers like "2,048" and "384" are strong evidence that this mathematical problem is hard. In the end, the word "though" indicates a worse situation, justifying the claim.

Get started on your own

Directions: Read Paragraph 13 carefully and write an analysis paragraph based on argument construction.

篇章分析

The article begins with an introduction of quantum computing which is likely to break cryptography in the future. This daunting trend is what cryptographer is working against. Possible countermeasures are proposed including information theory-based cryptography which might serve as the last resort. Perhaps this is what cryptography will be like after aliens land. Moving on, the author goes to lengths to explain why such a remedy is solid enough. By recapping core issues like asymmetry and how to encrypt as well as introducing the rationale of symmetric cryptography and public-key encryption, he argues why reversing the algorithm is currently beyond the reach of mankind. However, quantum computing can dismantle problems regarding symmetric cryptography and public-key encryption. Though for the former, Grove's algorithm has not yet to pose threat; Shor's algorithm can break the latter effectively. The harsh reality ridden with uncertainties and unknowns may sap what it is expected. Conversely, cryptography is secure for the time being despite that the expert worries that it will be completely broken deep down. Then comes the question of how to adapt to the shattered world. Several design possibilities are presented to set our mind at ease. Back to the number-theory based encryption which the public-key system relies on, it will be replaced by quantum key distribution one day yet it requires hardware, making it hard to be applicable. Hardwares like a quantum computer aside, cryptography based on information theory will be a blow to security. This communicating device using one-time pads will be the saviour of our world.

We visualize the text structure by means of a mind map.

Cryptography after the Aliens Land

- **Introduction to quantum computing (Paras. 1 - 2)**
- **Current cryptographic technologies (Paras. 3 - 7)**
  - Basics of current cryptographic technologies (Paras. 3 - 4)
  - Symmetric cryptography (Para. 5)
  - Public-key encryption (Para. 6)
  - One-wayness of current methods (Para. 7)
- **Challenges of current cryptographic technologies (Paras. 8 - 18)**
  - Quantum computing (Paras. 8 - 15)
    - Threats brought by quantum computing (Paras. 8 - 9)
    - Uncertainties and unknowns of quantum computing (Paras. 10 - 11)
    - Possible solutions (Paras. 12 - 15)
  - Future challenges (Paras. 16 - 18)
    - Symmetric cryptography to rely on (Para. 16)
    - One-time pads as the last resort (Paras. 17 - 18)

课堂提问

- How much do you know about quantum computing?
- What is the difference between symmetric cryptography and public-key encryption?
- What will the future be like if cryptography is completely broken?

教学建议

Apart from the first 6 paragraphs, the author poses a lot of questions and gives possible answers accordingly. Identify these questions and find out how the author responds to and evaluates them.

B. 课堂讨论模块

学习时间

2 hours

讨论内容

- To talk about security problems in the digital age.
- To share your view on future cryptography.
- To discuss the application of quantum computing in real life.

教学方法

heuristic teaching; group discussion; class presentation

组织形式

➢ Work in groups to present a slideshow about cryptography.

参考问题

➢ How can we protect our personal information in the digital age?

➢ What will cryptography be like in the future?

➢ How much do you know about quantum computing?

课后练习

Refer to the exercises in Unit Eight of the textbook.

练习答案

Part 1 Reading Comprehension

1. Directions: The reading passage has 18 paragraphs. Which paragraph contains the following information? Write the correct number, 1 - 18, in blanks 1)- 5).

1) Para. 2 2) Para. 7 3) Para. 9 4) Para. 16 5) Para. 17

2. Directions: Paraphrase the following sentences.

1) It's easy to make symmetric cryptography resist quantum attack. (Para. 2)

2) We use key lengths longer than necessary, in the hope of resisting future attacks as technology develops. (Para. 7)

3) If we double the key length for public-key cryptography, the difficulty to break it will increase by a factor of eight. (Para. 9)

4) The security relies on centralized points, compromising which will lead to the collapse of the whole systems. (Para. 13)

5) If the future is dominated by aliens as in the science fiction, we might have no cryptography to protect us. (Para. 17)

Part 2 Words and Expressions

3. Directions: Choose proper words from the following word bank, and fill in blanks in their right forms.

1) underpins 2) dire 3) Astronomical 4) nascent 5) unsurmountable
6) quirk 7) detour 8) conceivable 9) upend 10) muddle

Part 3 Translation

4. Directions: Translate the following sentences from the reading passage into Chinese.

1) 正如打碎盘子要比把碎盘子粘好容易，把两个素数相乘得到大数也要比把同一个大数分解成两个素数容易得多。

2) Grover 算法证明量子计算可使攻击加速，从而有效缩短一半密钥长度。这意味着，256 比特密钥抗量子计算机攻击和 128 比特密钥抗传统计算机攻击的强度相当，二者在可预见的将来都是安全的。

3) 我打赌工程难题终将被跨越，新技术、新进展会层出不穷，但其发现、发明尚需时日。正如超级计算机历经数十载风雨才缩小到可以放入口袋，要搭建足够大的量子计算机，有必要一一攻克所有工程难题，而这也得花上几十年时间。

4) 对称密码搅混信息的方式如此之非线性，轻而易举就可以增加密钥长度和复杂度，其未来不可限量。想想一个分组、密钥长度均为 512 比特的 128 轮 AES 变体吧，其安全性将无从挑战，除非数学本质被彻底颠覆，或者直到有一天，计算机既不由物质构成，也不用空间存放。

5) 现在，只有疯子才会去设计基于一次一密的通用体制，密码学家也对他们嘲笑不已，因为简单的算法设计问题变成了复杂得多的密钥管理和物理安全问题。然而，如果未来真如科幻小说般被外星人占领，除了一次一密我们又能剩下什么呢？

Part 4 Sentence Structure

5. Directions: Combine the following sentences in each group into a complex sentence.

1) If it did, it would open up its diversity program, now focused narrowly on race and gender, and look for reporters who differ broadly by outlook, values, education, and class.

2) On another level, many in the medical community acknowledge that the assisted—suicide debate has been fueled in part by the despair of patients for whom modern medicine has prolonged the physical agony of dying.

3) I believe that the most important forces behind the massive merge and acquisition wave are the same that underlie the globalization process: falling transportation and communication costs, lower trade and investment barriers and enlarged markets that require enlarged operations capable of meeting customers' demands.

4) Nor, if regularity and conformity to a standard pattern are as desirable to the scientist as the writing of his papers would appear to reflect, is management to be blamed for discriminating against the "odd balls" among researchers in favor of more conventional thinkers who "work well with the team".

5) The paid manager acting for the company was in more direct relation with the men and their demands, but even he had seldom that familiar personal knowledge of the workmen which the employer had often had under the more patriarchal system of the old family business now passing away.

Part 5 Academic Writing Skills

6. Directions: Use the following elements in each group to write a sentence showing "similarity" "dissimilarity" or "superiority and inferiority" in comparison, or showing "contrast".

1) The non-parametric methods *are rather less efficient than* their semi-parametric counterparts under a correctly specified model.

2) The efficiency of LCL-VSC *is similar to* that of the conventional L-VSC.

3) *Different from/In contrast to/As opposed to* other methods, the proposed method has no special requirements for encryption algorithms, which makes it more universal and fit for application in different scenarios.
4) The grid cells are used to represent the surface characteristics of different regions, *whereas* the grid edges are used to measure the flux relationships between cells.
5) The algorithm proposed in this paper *is superior to* current methodology for detecting structural change.
6) The LTE power model *differs from* all aforementioned models in two aspects.
7) The results are *as accurate as* the theory predicated.
8) The estimates obtained from Headrick's algorithm *are less biased than* the estimates obtained through Vale and Maurelli.
9) Short-term effects *may be more harmful than* long-term errors.
10) When computational heterogeneity is high, the eFRD algorithm *becomes inferior to* the FGLS algorithm.

Unit Nine
Deep Learning

Section A From Not Working to Neural Networking

文章主旨

This article tells us the origin of deep learning, its different categories, and its current development and future.

教学目标

➢ To gain a clear understanding of deep learning.

➢ To master the technical words and expressions related to deep learning.

➢ To be able to use the knowledge learned to discuss issues about deep learning.

学习时间

4 hours (2 hours for the text; 2 hours for discussion)

A. 课堂讲授模块

预习要求

➢ To learn and recite the new words.

➢ To grasp the main idea of the text after reading.

➢ To search for materials related to deep learning.

学习时间

2 hours

教学方法

heuristic teaching; project-based teaching; task-driven teaching; group discussion; self-study and peer learning

组织形式

- Let the students work in groups to discuss the text structure and its main idea based on fast reading, and to draw a simple mind-map as well.
- Summarize key technical terms, words and phrases, and sentence patterns in articles involving such technologies as AI, deep learning, etc.
- Let students discuss in groups the learning gains based on their fields of research, and a presentation is expected.
- Analyze the complex sentences and technical issues. Spare some time to respond to any questions from the students.

背景知识

1. Deep Learning

Deep Learning is a new area of Machine Learning research, which has been introduced with the objective of moving Machine Learning closer to one of its original goals: Artificial Intelligence. Instead of organizing data to run through predefined equations, deep learning sets up basic parameters about the data and trains the computer to learn on its own by recognizing patterns using many layers of processing. Deep learning techniques have improved the ability of the computer to perform human-like tasks, such as recognizing speech, identifying images, making predictions, and describing contents. Systems such as Siri and Cortana are powered, in part, by deep learning.

2. Artificial Neural Network (ANN)

An artificial neural network (ANN), usually called neural network (NN), is a mathematical model or computational model that is inspired by the structure and/or functional aspects of biological neural networks. A neural network consists of an interconnected group of artificial neurons, and it processes information using a connectionist approach to computation. In most cases an ANN is an adaptive system that changes its structure based on external or internal information that flows through the network during the learning phase. Modern neural networks are non-linear statistical data modeling tools. They are usually used to model complex relationships between inputs and outputs or to find patterns in data.

The core component of ANNs is artificial neurons. Each neuron receives inputs from several other neurons, multiplies them by assigned weights, adds them and passes the sum to one or more neurons. Some artificial neurons might apply an activation function to the output before passing it to the next variable.

Artificial neural networks are composed of an input layer, which receives data from outside sources (data files, images, hardware sensors, microphone ...), one or more hidden layers that process the data, and an output layer that provides one or more data points based on the function of the network. For instance, a neural network that detects persons, cars and animals will have an output layer with three nodes. A network that classifies bank transactions between safe and fraudulent will have a single output.

3. DeepMind

DeepMind is a London-based company, owned by Google, which is developing artificial intelligence programs. DeepMind first came into the spotlight when it developed a program capable of learning how to play video games. The simple program managed to beat 49 different titles on an old Atari console, at the same level a human would be able to. It then made headlines in 2016 when one of its programs, AlphaGo, defeated a world champion Go player. This was something that had never been achieved before. The historic moment AlphaGo defeated 18-time world champion Lee Sedol is often compared to the 1997 match between chess master Gary Kasparov and Deep Blue the computer.

4. MetaMind

MetaMind is a Palo Alto-based AI startup founded in July 2014. MetaMind's general-purpose platform was designed to predict outcomes for language, vision, and database tasks.

5. Artificial General Intelligence

AI can be broken down into three stages: artificial narrow intelligence (ANI), artificial general intelligence (AGI) and artificial super intelligence (ASI).

Artificial narrow intelligence is a weak AI that involves machines that are capable to perform only a narrow set of specified tasks. The machines at this stage do not have the ability to think; rather they just perform a set of predefined tasks.

Artificial general intelligence is a strong AI where machines will be capable to think, make decisions, solve puzzles, learn and communicate just like human beings. There are no currently existing examples of AGI; however, in the future, humans will be able to create a machine that is smart as a human being. The evolution of this stage is considered to many as a threat to human existence.

Artificial super intelligence is a stage of evolution of AI where the machines are capable to surpass human beings. Currently, ASI is a hypothetical scenario as shown in movies and fiction reading material where machines have taken over the world.

6. Smart Reply

Smart Reply is a new feature in Google's Inbox app which can recognize the content of emails and tailor responses using natural language. Machine learning is used to scan emails and understand if they need replying to or not. An email asking about vacation plans, for example, could be replied to with "No plans yet" "I just sent them to you" or "I'm working on them".

Smart Reply is built on a pair of recurrent neural networks, one that encodes incoming emails and one that comes up with possible responses. Each word is captured in turn to create a list of numbers, known as a thought vector that gives the machine learning system the gist of what is being said. From this, the second network builds a grammatically correct response one word at a time.

重点词汇

1. **hubris** /ˈhjuːbrɪs / *n*. excessive pride or self-confidence 傲慢
   - ➢ How has artificial intelligence, associated with ***hubris*** and disappointment since its earliest days, suddenly become the hottest field in technology? (Para. 1)
   - ➢ But here his own ***hubris***, his own kind of arrogance, in how to handle this matter prevailed.
2. **surpass** /səˈpɑːs/ *v*. exceed; be greater than 超过
   - ➢ This brought further rapid improvements, producing an accuracy of 96% in the ImageNet Challenge in 2015 and ***surpassing*** humans for the first time. (Para. 2)
   - ➢ The sound for the game, however, far ***surpasses*** any expectation for a video game.
3. **trigger** /ˈtrɪɡə/ *v*. cause (an event or situation) to happen or exist 引起
   - ➢ In a biological brain, each neuron can be ***triggered*** by other neurons whose outputs feed into it, and its own output can then trigger other neurons in turn. (Para. 4)
   - ➢ Observers saw the message as a strong hint that ***triggered*** the following events.
4. **tweak** /twiːk/ *n*. a fine adjustment to a mechanism or system 改进
   - ➢ In the past decade new techniques and a simple ***tweak*** to the activation function have made training deep networks feasible. (Para. 5)
   - ➢ The technology is still in need of some ***tweaks*** and adjustments, but nothing is perfect straight from prototype.
5. **domain** /dəʊˈmeɪn/ *n*. a specified sphere of activity or knowledge 领域
   - ➢ "What got people excited about this field is that one learning technique, deep learning, can be applied to so many different ***domains***," says John Giannandrea, head of machine-intelligence research at Google and now in charge of its search engine too. (Para. 7)
   - ➢ In this ***domain***, as with so much modern technology, people are not just consumers; they're producers.
6. **anomaly** /əˈnɒm(ə)li/ *n*. something that deviates from what is standard, normal, or expected 异常
   - ➢ Unsupervised learning can be used to search for things when you do not know what they look like: for monitoring network traffic patterns for ***anomalies*** that might correspond to a cyber-attack, for example, or examining large numbers of

insurance claims to detect new kinds of fraud. (Para. 11)

➢ Field workers are currently investigating another ***anomaly*** that turned up in the survey.

7. **distil** /dɪˈstɪl/ *v*. extract the essential meaning or most important aspects of 提炼

➢ On the screen was a furry face, a pattern ***distilled*** from thousands of examples. (Para. 11)

➢ By this time, results from years of research and analysis had been ***distilled***.

8. **generate** /ˈdʒenəreɪt/ *v*. produce or create 造成

➢ In essence, training involves adjusting the network's weights to search for a strategy that consistently ***generates*** higher rewards. (Para. 12)

➢ It would be a place for ideas to be ***generated*** and developed to create new products and services within the digital industry.

9. **ingest** /ɪnˈdʒest/ *v*. take (food, drink, or another substance) into the body by swallowing or absorbing it 摄取

➢ Like DeepMind, it is exploring modular architectures; one them, called a "dynamic memory network", can, among other things, ***ingest*** a series of statements and then answer questions about them, deducing the logical connections between them. (Para. 16)

➢ The archive connects to the applications and ***ingests*** the stream of information that comes from that source.

10. **ream** /riːm/ *n*. (usually reams) a large quantity of something, especially paper or writing 大量的

➢ A more cynical view is that big internet firms can afford to give away their AI software because they have a huge advantage elsewhere: access to ***reams*** of user data for training purposes. (Para. 19)

➢ But he also wrote ***reams*** of unpublished serious music.

11. **edge** /edʒ/ *n*. a quality or factor which gives superiority over close rivals 优势

➢ This gives them an ***edge*** in particular areas, says Shivon Zilis of Bloomberg Beta, an investment fund, but startups are finding ways into specific markets. (Para. 19)

➢ Its quick reaction time and high rate of fire gives the Indian Army an ***edge*** during low intensity war-like situations.

12. **incremental** /ˌɪŋkrəˈmentl/ *adj*. relating to or denoting an increase or addition, especially one of a series on a fixed scale 增加的

➢ To most people, all this progress in AI will manifest itself as ***incremental*** improvements to internet services they already use every day. (Para. 21)

➢ Most research proceeds by small ***incremental*** advances.

13. **embed** /ɪmˈbed/ *v*. design and build (a microprocessor) as an integral part of a

system or device 嵌入

- Within a few years everything will have intelligence ***embedded*** in it to some extent, predicts Mr. Hassabis. (Para. 21)
- A small microchip is ***embedded*** into a debit or credit card and provides both highly secure memory and complex processing capabilities.

14. accelerate /əkˈseləreɪt/ *v*. increase in rate, amount, or extent 加速

- "Steam has fearfully ***accelerated*** a process that was going on already, but too fast," declared Robert Southey, an English poet. (Para. 23)
- Throughout 2003 the monthly increases in the unemployment rate ***accelerated*** and the average number of hours worked declined.

重点短语

1. end up: to reach or come to a place, condition, or situation that was not planned or expected 最终成为

- Researchers mostly ***ended up*** avoiding the term, preferring to talk instead about "expert systems" or "neural networks". (Para. 1)
- She'll ***end up*** penniless if she continues to spend like that.
- We moved around a lot when I was young but we ***ended up*** in London.

2. trace (back) to: to find the origin or cause of something 追溯

- The rehabilitation of "AI", and the current excitement about the field, can ***be traced back to*** 2012 and an online contest called the ImageNet Challenge. (Para. 1)
- The outbreak of food poisoning ***was traced to*** some contaminated shellfish.
- The practice of giving eggs at Easter can ***be traced back to*** festivals in ancient China.

3. in essence: relating to the most important characteristics or ideas of something 本质上

- ***In essence***, this technique uses huge amounts of computing power and vast quantities of training data to supercharge an old idea from the dawn of AI: so-called artificial neural networks (ANNs). (Para. 3)
- Because ***in essence***, power is getting other people to accept your interpretation of things.
- To wish it were otherwise is ***in essence*** to wish that we were not physical beings at all.

4. conjure up: to make a picture or idea appear in someone's mind 想象出

- It is a pleasing symmetry, says Jen-Hsun Huang, the boss of NVIDIA, which makes GPUs, that the same chips that are used to ***conjure up*** imaginary worlds for gamers can also be used to help computers understand the real world through deep learning. (Para. 5)
- The glittering ceremony ***conjured up*** images of Russia's imperial past.

> However, her pictures are not about the romantic images that these ***conjure up***, but focus on the world they transport the viewer too.

5. **work through**: to deal with (something that is difficult or unpleasant) successfully 逐步解决(困难的)问题

> A deep-learning system can be trained using this database, repeatedly ***working through*** the examples and adjusting the weights inside the neural network to improve its accuracy in assessing spamminess. (Para. 8)

> It's a complex situation but we'll ***work through*** it.

> He saw a psychologist to help him ***work through*** his depression.

6. **draw up**: to make or write something that needs careful thought or planning 草拟

> The great merit of this approach is that there is no need for a human expert to ***draw up*** a list of rules, or for a programmer to implement them in code; the system learns directly from the labeled data. (Para. 8)

> Make sure the contract is properly ***drawn up***.

> A specification has been ***drawn up*** for the new military aircraft.

7. **in between**: between two clear or accepted stages or states, and therefore difficult to describe or know exactly 介于两者之间

> Reinforcement learning sits somewhere ***in between*** supervised and unsupervised learning. (Para. 12)

> There were pieces everywhere and blank spaces ***in between***.

> The small space ***in between*** allowed a continuous flow of air to ventilate the rooms below.

8. **from scratch**: from the very beginning, especially without utilizing or relying on any previous work for assistance 从头开始

> The system learned to play them all ***from scratch*** and achieved human-level performance or better in 29 of them. (Para. 12)

> He built his own computer company ***from scratch***.

> Native programmers are used to support or maintain current systems, not to produce new ones ***from scratch***.

9. **run out of steam**: to lose one's energy, motivation, or enthusiasm to continue doing something 失去动力

> In the past, promising new AI techniques have tended to ***run out of steam*** quickly. (Para. 17)

> The peace talks seem to have ***run out of steam***.

> The two very sexy stars provide enough chemistry in this stylized thriller but the movie ***runs out of steam*** halfway through.

10. **aspire to**: to have a strong wish or hope to do or have something 有志于

> The long-term goal ***to*** which Mr. Hassabis, Mr. Socher and others ***aspire*** is to

build an "artificial general intelligence" (AGI)—a system capable of solving a wide range of tasks—rather than building a new AI system for each problem. (Para. 17)

- He quickly reached standards of musicianship that the rest of us can only ***aspire to***.
- Few people who ***aspire to*** fame ever achieve it.

11. a dozen or so: about a dozen 十几个

- We think we know what the ***dozen or so*** key things are that are required to get us close to something like AGI. (Para. 17)
- The extension to a wider base has won them ***a dozen or so*** valuable new clients.
- Australian languages divide into ***a dozen or so*** families.

难句解析

1. All this takes a lot of number-crunching power, which became readily available when several AI research groups realized around 2009 that graphical processing units (GPUs), the specialized chips used in PCs and video-games consoles to generate fancy graphics, were also well suited to running deep-learning algorithms. (Para. 5)

Paraphrase: For all this, a lot of computing power is required, which became attainable in around 2009 when several AI research groups found that it is suitable to use graphics processing units (GPUs), the specialized chips used in PCs and video games consoles to generate beautiful graphics, to run deep learning algorithm.

解析：全句主干是 All this takes a lot of number-crunching power。后面的 which 引导非限制性定语从句修饰 number-crunching power。该从句中有一个 when 引导的时间状语从句，the specialized chips 为同位语，对 GPU 做出解释。限制性定语从句的关系词前不加逗号，非限制性定语从句应在关系词前加逗号。在限制性定语从句中，从句对被修饰的先行词有限定制约作用。限制性定语从句不能被省略，否则句意就不完整。在非限制性定语从句中，从句对先行词只是起补充说明作用，去掉也不会影响全句的理解。非限制性定语从句还可修饰整个主句。举例如下：

- He has a son ***who works in a university***. 他有一个在大学工作的儿子。(限制性的，可能还有别的儿子，但不在大学工作)
- He has a son, ***who works in a university***. 他有一个儿子，在大学工作。(只有这么一个儿子，非限制性，补充说明在大学工作)
- I will wear no clothes ***which will distinguish me from the others***. 我将不穿会使我与众不同的衣服。(限制性)
- I will wear no clothes, ***which will distinguish me from the others***. 我将不穿衣服，这样会使我与众不同。(非限制性)

翻译：所有这一切都需要大量的数字运算能力。当几个人工智能(AI)研究小组在2009年左右意识到图形处理单元(GPU)——用于个人电脑(PC)和视频游戏机来生成精美图形的专用芯片——也很适合运行深度学习算法，这种能力就变得唾手可得了。

2. An AI research group at Stanford University led by Andrew Ng, who subsequently moved to Google and now works for Baidu, a Chinese internet giant, found that GPUs could speed up its deep-learning system nearly a hundredfold. (Para. 5)

Paraphrase: An AI research group at Stanford University led by Andrew Ng (who later moved to Google and now works for a Chinese internet giant Baidu) found that GPUs can make deep-learning system nearly one hundred times faster.

解析：本句话的主语为 an AI research group，谓语为 found，中间 who 引导非限制性定语从句对 Andrew Ng 进行补充说明，a Chinese internet giant 为 Baidu 的同位语，补充说明 Baidu。当两个词或词组在一个句子中具有相同的语法地位而且描述相同的人或事物时，我们称它们为同位语。同位语与其同位成分通常用逗号隔开，还可以用括号和破折号隔开。同位语与其同位成分关系紧密时也可以不用逗号隔开。同位语的前面还会加上 namely, that is, in other words, i.e. 等引出介绍的词。举例如下：

➢ The long-term goal to which Mr. Hassabis, Mr. Socher and others aspire is to build an "artificial general intelligence" (AGI)—***a system capable of solving a wide range of tasks***—rather than building a new AI system for each problem. (Para. 17)

➢ He told me that his brother ***John*** was a famous scientist.

➢ My brother often likens himself to Zeus (***the god of thunder***).

➢ There is but one law for all, ***namely***, that law which governs all law, the law of our Creator, the law of humanity, justice and equity—the law of nature and of nations.

翻译：斯坦福大学一个由吴恩达领导的人工智能研究小组发现，GPU 可以将其深度学习系统的速度提高近一百倍。吴恩达后来加入了谷歌，现在为中国互联网巨头百度工作。

3. Instead, the network learns to recognize features and cluster similar examples, thus revealing hidden groups, links or patterns within the data. (Para. 10)

Paraphrase: Instead, the network can reveal hidden groups, links or patterns within the data by learning to recognize features and assemble similar examples.

解析：现在分词短语 revealing ... 作结果状语。thus, therefore 和 so 意思接近，均有"因此"的意思，但 therefore 和 thus 比 so 更加正式。thus 和 therefore 都是副词，不能连接两个句子。而 so 则可以是连词，连接两个句子。通常情况下 thus 和 therefore 后面逗号均可省略。举例如下：

➢ He is not satisfied, ***so*** we must prepare a new proposal. (正确)

➢ He is not satisfied. ***Thus***, we must prepare a new proposal. (正确)

➢ He is not satisfied with it, ***thus*** we must prepare a new proposal. (错误，因为 thus 不能连接两个句子)

➢ The two lines intersect; ***therefore***, they are not parallel. (正确)

➢ He is not satisfied, and ***thus*** we must prepare a new proposal.（正确）

翻译：相反，网络学会识别特征并将相似的例子聚类，从而揭示数据中的隐藏的组、链接或模式。

4. In February 2015 it published a paper in *Nature* describing a reinforcement-learning system capable of learning to play 49 classic Atari video games, using just the on-screen pixels and the game score as inputs, with its output connected to a virtual controller.（Para. 12）

Paraphrase：In February 2015 it published a paper in Nature. This paper introduced a reinforcement-learning system which can learn to play 49 classic Atari video games, with only the on-screen pixels and the game score as inputs and output connected to a virtual controller.

解析：句中现在分词短语 using ... 和 with 复合结构作状语，补充说明这个 reinforcement-learning system。with 复合结构可放在句首或句尾，通常在句中作时间、原因、方式和伴随状语。with 复合结构的基本形式为 with/without＋宾语＋宾语补足语。举例如下：

➢ ***With*** a lot of work ***to do***, he wasn't allowed to go out.（with＋名词/代词＋不定式）

➢ She is also five feet five inches tall ***with*** a scar ***under her nose*** and brown hair.（with＋名词/代词＋介词短语）

➢ He lay on his back, ***with*** his teeth ***set*** and his eyes ***closed***.（with＋名词/代词＋过去分词短语）

➢ ***With*** the machine ***helping us***, we finished the work.（with＋名词/代词＋现在分词短语）

➢ ***With*** the weather so ***close*** and ***stuffy***, ten to one it'll rain presently.（with＋名词/代词＋形容词）

➢ I've been sleeping ***with*** the lights ***on***, talking in my sleep and waking to an empty home.（with＋名词/代词＋副词）

翻译：2015 年 2 月，该公司在《自然》杂志上发表了一篇论文，描述了一个强化学习系统，该系统能够学习玩 49 款经典雅达利（Atari）电子游戏，仅使用屏幕像素和游戏分数作为输入，其输出与一个虚拟控制器相连。

5. Others are worried, fearing that AI technology could supercharge the existing computerization and automation of certain tasks, just as steam power, along with new kinds of machinery, seemed poised to make many workers redundant 200 years ago.（Para. 23）

Paraphrase：Two hundred years ago, steam power and new kinds of machinery make many workers lose their jobs. Now, some people worried that AI might do a similar thing for its excessive computerization and automation of certain tasks.

解析：本句中现在分词短语 fearing ... 补充说明担心的事情是什么。后面 just as 引导方式状语从句，意思为“正如……”。along with ... 为插入语。插入语是指插在句子中对其他句子成分作补充说明的单词、短语或句子（同位语为插入语的一种），通常由逗号、破折号和括号与主句隔开。插入语在语法上与句子的其他成分没有关系，不充当句子成分，去掉完全不影响句子结构。举例如下：

➢ Like DeepMind, it is exploring modular architectures; one them, called a "dynamic memory network", can, ***among other things***, ingest a series of statements and then answer questions about them, deducing the logical connections between them (Kermit is a frog; frogs are green; so Kermit is green). (Para. 16)

➢ The old man, ***it is said***, was an artist but people hardly know anything about this side of his life.

➢ The party lasted—***we knew it would***! —far longer than planned.

➢ The tone of her letter, ***however***, brought tears to Fang's eyes.

➢ He was (***strange as it seems***) an excellent sportsman.

翻译：其他人则担心人工智能技术会加速现有的某些任务的计算机化和自动化，就像200年前蒸汽动力和新型机械导致许多工人下岗一样。

写作技巧

Punctuation

Overview

Punctuation marks are very important. They show readers where sentences start and finish. Without punctuation, it would be very difficult to understand any piece of writing. Using punctuation appropriately is very essential in English writing. Like many of the so-called "laws" of grammar, there are many rules for using punctuation. In the following part are rules of some punctuation.

➢ **Hyphen**(-)

The primary function of a hyphen is the formation of certain compound terms. We can find many examples in this article, such as so-called, number-crunching, machine-intelligence, deep-learning etc.

Another function of the hyphen is to divide words at the end of a line in professionally printed material. If it is required by publication, please split the words appropriately, generally between different syllables, for example la-bel instead of lab-el, sen-tence instead of sent-ence.

➢ **En Dash**(–)

An en dash is longer than a hyphen and shorter than an em dash. It is used to represent a range of numbers, dates, or time. There should be no space on both sides of an en dash. Depending on the context, the en dash should be read as "to" or "through".

➢ Write the correct number (1 – 28) on the answer sheet.

If you use words like *from* or *between* to introduce the range, do not use the en dash. For example:

➢ She studied in IEU from 1999 to 2003. (√)

➢ She studied in IEU from 1999 – 2003. (×)

➢ **Em Dash (—)**

The em dash indicates added emphasis, an interruption, or an abrupt change of thought. It can replace punctuation marks like commas, parentheses, or colons. Em dashes are generally used in informal writing. AP style calls for a space on both sides of an em dash; but most other styles, including MLA and APA, omit the spaces.

➢ It consists of several interconnected modules, including two deep neural networks, each of which specializes in a different thing—just like the modules of the human brain. (Para. 14)

➢ The dynamic nature of deep learning methods—their ability to continuously improve and adapt to changes in the underlying information pattern—presents a great opportunity to introduce more dynamic behavior into analytics. (Text B)

Usually, comma and parentheses can be used to take place of the em dash. The above two examples can also be written as follows.

➢ It consists of several interconnected modules, including two deep neural networks, each of which specializes in a different thing, just like the modules of the human brain.

➢ The dynamic nature of deep learning methods (their ability to continuously improve and adapt to changes in the underlying information pattern) presents a great opportunity to introduce more dynamic behavior into analytics.

➢ **Parentheses ( )**

Parentheses are used in pairs to provide additional or explanatory information. The information inside the parentheses does not interrupt the flow of a sentence. Contents enclosed in parentheses generally include additional information, numbers or letters, give in-text citations/reference information, or provide abbreviations and acronyms or full terms. The following are some examples.

➢ In 2010 the winning system could correctly label an image 72% of the time (for humans, the average is 95%). (Para. 2)

➢ Please submit the following four items with your application: (1) a cover letter, (2) a resume, (3) a college transcript, and (4) a list of professional references.

➢ In order to explore such a work environment, the Remembrance Agent (Rhodes and Starner, 1996) was created.

➢ In essence, this technique uses huge amounts of computing power and vast quantities of training data to supercharge an old idea from the dawn of AI: so-called artificial neural networks (ANNs). (Para. 3)

Note that the parenthetical content is not grammatically integral to the surrounding sentence. If the parenthetical material is removed, a sentence should remain grammatically correct.

➢ Joe (and his colleague) **is** expected to arrive at 9:00 a.m.

If a complete parenthetical sentence is at the end of a sentence, a period should be placed inside the parentheses and it is also acceptable that no period is used inside the parentheses. The parenthetical sentence should not be capitalized if no punctuation is enclosed in the parentheses.

➢ A simple ANN has an input layer of neurons where data can be fed into the network, an output layer where results come out, and possibly a couple of hidden layers in the middle where information is processed. (In practice, ANNs are simulated entirely in software.) (Para. 4)

➢ In 2010 the winning system could correctly label an image 72% of the time (for humans, the average is 95%). (Para. 2)

Punctuate correctly when using punctuation.

➢ MetaMind has also combined natural-language and image-recognition networks into a single system that can answer questions about images ("What color is the car?"). (Para. 16)

If the parenthetical sentence is in the middle of a sentence, no punctuation should be enclosed and surrounding punctuation should be placed outside and after the parentheses.

➢ We verified his law degree (none of us thought he was lying about that) but not his billion-dollar verdict against Exxon.

➢ When he got home (it was already dark outside), he finished dinner.

➢ **Semi Colon (;)**

A semi colon is stronger than a comma, but weaker than a period. It is generally used to separate independent clauses that share the same idea. Semi colons are used between two independent clauses (i.e., clauses that could stand alone as separate sentences) without a coordinating conjunction (for, and, nor, but, or, yet, so). Semi colons are also used between two independent clauses linked by a conjunctive adverb (such as however or therefore) or a transitional expression (e.g., in fact, for example, accordingly, consequently, that is, for instance etc.).

➢ There is a steady flow of academic papers from AI companies both large and small; AI researchers have been allowed to continue publishing their results in peer-reviewed journals, even after moving into industry. (Para. 18)

➢ For the final phase, the department's plan calls for an initial purchase of 8 GPS Ⅲ C satellites, which will be equipped with a special antenna capable of focusing the M-code signals in a "spotbeam"; however, CBO assumes that the department would need to purchase an additional 8 Ⅲ C satellites in order to have enough Ⅲ C satellites in orbit to take advantage of the Ⅲ C's advanced capabilities. (Para. 5, Section A, Unit 3)

➢ To a large extent, the future of the Internet of Things will not be possible without the support of IPv6; and consequently, the global adoption of IPv6 in the coming years will be critical for the successful development of the IoT in the future. (Section B, Unit 4)

A semi colon is also used to separate items of a series when these items contain commas to prevent confusion.

➢ I met Mr. Liu, chief executive officer; Mr. Guo, chief financial officer; Linda, chief operating officer.

And remember do not capitalize the letter after a semi colon.

Get started on your own

Directions: Read the following sentences carefully and analyze the usage of the punctuation.

1. Facebook can recognize and tag your friends and family when you upload a photograph, and recently launched a system that describes the contents of photographs for blind users ("two people, smiling, sunglasses, outdoor, water").
2. "I remember him calling me over to his computer and saying, 'look at this'," Mr. Ng recalls.
3. Deep learning techniques have improved the ability to classify, recognize, detect and describe—in one word, understand.
4. Self-driving cars are getting better fast; at some point soon they may be able to replace taxi drivers, at least in controlled environments such as city centers.
5. While talking to you, I have occasionally watched Adèle (I have my own reasons for thinking her a curious study—reasons that I may, nay, that I shall impart to you some day).

篇章分析

This article addresses the hottest field in technology: artificial intelligence (AI). From not working to neural networking, the rehabitation of AI can be traced back to the 2012 ImageNet Challenge, in which "deep learning" is first used to recognize and label images automatically. Deep learning technique can be classified into three main categories: supervised learning, unsupervised learning and reinforcement learning. Supervised learning involves training a system to recognize patterns with the aid of labeled examples, while unsupervised learning involves training with a huge number of unlabeled examples to find patterns. Reinforcement learning is somewhere in between them, which involves training a neural network with only occasional feedback as a reward. One famous reinforcement-learning system is AlphaGo of DeepMind, which defeated a world champion Go player. Now, AI companies like DeepMind and MetaMind are exploring new technologies, such as transfer learning, and multitask learning, to make AI more useful to human beings. However, some worry that the powerful AI will be a threat to human beings in terms of employment.

We visualize the text structure by means of a mind map.

From Not Working to Neural Networking

- **Rehabitation of AI (Paras. 1 – 7)**
  - Rehabitation of AI: deep learning (Paras. 1 – 5)
  - Promising applications of AI (Paras. 6 – 7)
- **Learning how to learn (Paras. 8 – 12)**
  - Supervised learning (Paras. 8 – 9)
  - Unsupervised learning (Paras. 10 – 11)
  - Reinforcement learning(Para. 12)
- **Gaming the system (Paras. 13 – 19)**
  - Research of DeepMind (Paras. 13 – 15)
  - Research of MetaMind (Para. 16)
  - Research prospect (Paras. 17 – 19)
- **Pick and mix (Paras. 20 – 23)**
  - Progress made (Para. 20)
  - Advantages of deep learning (Paras. 21 – 22)
  - Threats of deep learning (Para. 23)

课堂提问

- What do you know about AI?
- Can you tell the differences between supervised learning and unsupervised learning? (Paras. 8 – 11)
- What are the advantages and disadvantages of AI? (Paras. 22 – 23)

教学建议

This article introduces the origin of deep learning, its different categories, and its development. Language are quite simple but with some technical terms. Therefore, students are well advised to gain a better understanding of what is deep learning and master technical terms at the same time.

B. 课堂讨论模块

学习时间

2 hours

讨论内容

- To discuss the benefits and troubles that AI brings us.
- To use the words and expressions learned to discuss issues about AI.
- To use one's professional knowledge to predict the future of AI.

教学方法

heuristic teaching; group discussion; class presentation

组织形式

- Let the students as groups present a PPT about AI.
- Discuss their expectation of the future of AI in groups and then present their group's idea after discussion.

参考问题

- Can you describe different types of deep learning in your own words?
- What are the benefits and troubles that AI brings us?
- What do you think is the future of AI?
- Do you think AI will take our jobs away?

课后练习

Refer to the exercises in Unit Nine of the textbook.

练习答案

Part 1 Reading Comprehension

1. **Directions**: The reading passage has 23 paragraphs. Which paragraph contains the following information? Write the correct number, 1 - 23, in blanks 1 - 5).

   1) Para.2 2) Para.6 3) Para.9 4) Para.17 5) Para.20

2. **Directions**: Paraphrase the following sentences.

   1) Though there was occasional progress, AI didn't live up to its promises in most cases. (Para.1)

   2) It is pleasing that the same chips used to conjure up imaginary worlds for gamers can also be used to help computers understand the real world through deep learning. (Para.5)

   3) The experience gained through solving one problem could be learned and promote

the solving of another problem. (Para. 16)

4) Artificial intelligence can also expect to rely on modest amounts of data, just like humans do. (Para. 19)

5) Because of steam, the already ongoing process of machines replacing humans became too fast, and thus very frightening. (Para. 23)

Part 2 Words and Expressions

3. Directions: Choose proper words from the following word bank, and fill in blanks in their right forms.

1) readily 2) supercharge 3) fraudulent 4) microcosm 5) incubator

6) anomalies 7) follow-up 8) tweaks 9) incremental 10) hubris

Part 3 Translation

4. Directions: Translate the following sentences from the reading passage into Chinese.

1) 完成这一切都需要耗费大量计算能力。当几个人工智能(AI)研究小组在2009年左右意识到图形处理单元(GPU)——用于个人电脑(PC)和视频游戏机来生成精美图形的专用芯片——也很适合运行深度学习算法,这种能力就变得唾手可得了。

2) 谷歌正利用深度学习来改善其网络搜索结果的质量,帮助智能手机理解语音指令,在图库中搜索特定图片,为电子邮件推荐自动回信,提高网页翻译服务质量,并帮助无人驾驶汽车掌握周围环境。

3) 搜索自己心里都没谱的东西时,无监管学习就派得上用场了。例如,监控网络流量模式,以发现网络攻击可能对应的异常行为,或者通过审查大量保险索赔来判断是否有新型骗保行为。

4) 部分原因是研究人员想发布公司的研究进展,这有助于招募人才。更愤世嫉俗一点来看,这些大型互联网公司之所以免费开放自家的AI软件,是因为他们手握其他杀手锏:即能够获取大量用于训练的用户数据。

5) 然而量变会引发质变,一旦跨过临界点,机器就能够执行一些之前专属于人类的任务……迪克逊先生说,未来必定还会有更多让人意想不到的突破。

Part 4 Sentence Structure

5. Directions: Combine the following sentences in each group into a complex sentence.

1) Although it ruled that there is no constitutional right to physician-assisted suicide, the Court in effect supported the medical principle of "double effect", a centuries-old moral principle holding that an action having two effects—a good one that is intended and a harmful one that is foreseen—is permissible if the actor intends only the good effect.

2) A lateral move that hurt my pride and blocked my professional progress promoted me to abandon my relatively high profile career although, in the manner of a disgraced government minister, I covered my exit by claiming "I wanted to spend more time with my family".

3) Last year Mitsuo Setoyama, who was then education minister, raised eyebrows

when he argued that liberal reforms introduced by the American occupation authorities after World War Ⅱ had weakened the "Japanese morality of respect for parents".

4) When a new movement in art attains a certain fashion, it is advisable to find out what its advocates are aiming at, for, however farfetched and unreasonable their principles may seem today, it is possible that in years to come they may be regarded as normal.

5) An invisible border divides those arguing for computers in the classroom on the behalf of students' career prospects and those arguing for computers in the classroom for broader reasons of radical education reform.

Part 5 Academic Writing Skills

6. Directions: Fill in the blanks according to the given graph.

1) sharply 2) moderate 3) increase 4) peak 5) considerably
6) stabilized 7) upward 8) reached 9) showed 10) slightly
11) fluctuated 12) dropped

References

[1] JOHN L. College Writing Skills with Reading [M]. 8th ed. NY：McGraw-Hill, 2011.

[2] BO B, HE Z A. English Grammar [M]. Kaiming Press. 2003.

[3] Hornby A S. Oxford Advanced Learner's English-Chinese Dictionary [M]. The Commercial Press. 2018.

[4] Mayor M. Longman Dictionary of Contemporary English [M]. Pearson Education Limited, 2009.

[5] Ding W D, Wu B, Zhong M S, Guo Q Q. A Handbook of Writing [M]. Foreign Language Teaching and Research Press, 1994.

[6] Strunk W, White E B. The Elements of Style [M]. Penguin Books, 2007.

[7] WAYNE C B, GREGORY G C, JOSEPH M W. The Craft of Research [M]. 3rd ed. Chicago：University of Chicago Press, 2008.

[8] Richard Nordquist. An Introduction to Punctuation [DB/OL]. https://www.thoughtco.com/punctuation-definition-1691702.

[9] Free Online English Usage Rules. [DB/OL] https://www.grammarbook.com/.

[10] The Punctuation Guide. [DB/OL] https://www.thepunctuationguide.com/.

[11] 林易，曲婧华，张娅丽.研究生英语读写教程[M].上海：上海交通大学出版社，2020.